Percy Addleshaw

The Cathedral Church of Exeter

A description of its fabric and a brief history of the Episcopal See

Percy Addleshaw

The Cathedral Church of Exeter
A description of its fabric and a brief history of the Episcopal See

ISBN/EAN: 9783337260729

Printed in Europe, USA, Canada, Australia, Japan

Cover: Foto ©ninafisch / pixelio.de

More available books at **www.hansebooks.com**

BELL'S CATHEDRAL SERIES
EDITED BY
GLEESON WHITE AND EDWARD F. STRANGE

EXETER

BELL'S CATHEDRAL SERIES.

EDITED BY

GLEESON WHITE AND E. F. STRANGE.

In specially designed cloth cover, crown 8vo, 1s. 6d. each.

Now Ready.

CANTERBURY. By HARTLEY WITHERS. 2nd Edition, revised.
SALISBURY. By GLEESON WHITE.
CHESTER. By CHARLES HIATT.
ROCHESTER. By G. H. PALMER, B.A.
OXFORD. By the Rev. PERCY DEARMER, M.A.
EXETER. By PERCY ADDLESHAW, B.A.
LICHFIELD. By A. B. CLIFTON.
HEREFORD. By A. HUGH FISHER.
NORWICH. By C. H. B. QUENNELL.
PETERBOROUGH. By Rev. W. D. SWEETING.
WINCHESTER. By P. W. SERGEANT.

Preparing.

LINCOLN. By A. B. KENDRICK, B.A.
DURHAM. By J. E. BYGATE.
WELLS. By Rev. PERCY DEARMER, M.A.
ST. DAVID'S. By PHILIP ROBSON.
CHICHESTER. CARLISLE.
ST. ALBANS. ST. PAUL'S.

SOUTHWELL. By Rev. ARTHUR DIMOCK.
ELY. By T. D. ATKINSON.
WORCESTER. By E. F. STRANGE.
YORK. By A. CLUTTON BROCK, B.A.
BRISTOL. GLOUCESTER.
RIPON.

Uniform with the above Series.

BEVERLEY MINSTER. By CHARLES HIATT. [*Preparing.*

"For the purpose at which they aim they are admirably done, and there are few visitants to any of our noble shrines who will not enjoy their visit the better for being furnished with one of these delightful books, which can be slipped into the pocket and carried with ease, and is yet distinct and legible. . . ."—*Notes and Queries.*

"We have so frequently in these columns urged the want of cheap well-illustrated, and well-written handbooks to our cathedrals, to take the place of the out-of-date publications of local booksellers, that we are glad to hear that they have been taken in hand by Messrs. George Bell and Sons."—*St. James's Gazette.*

"Visitors to the cathedral cities of England must often have felt the need of some work dealing with the history and antiquities of the city itself, and the architecture and associations of the cathedral, more portable than the elaborate monographs which have been devoted to some of them, more scholarly and satisfying than the average local guide-book, and more copious than the section devoted to them in the general guide-book of the county or district. Such a legitimate need the 'Cathedral Series' now being issued by Messrs. George Bell and Sons under the editorship of Mr. Gleeson White and Mr. E. F. Strange seems well calculated to supply. The volumes are handy in size, moderate in price, well illustrated, and written in a scholarly spirit. The history of cathedral and city is intelligently set forth and accompanied by a descriptive survey of the building in all its detail. The illustrations are copious and well selected, and the series bids fair to become an indispensable companion to the cathedral tourist in England."—*Times.*

"They are nicely produced in good type, on good paper, and contain numerous illustrations, are well written, and very cheap. We should imagine architects and students of architecture will be sure to buy the series as they appear, for they contain in brief much valuable information."—*British Architect.*

"There is likely to be a large demand for these attractive handbooks."—*Globe.*

LONDON: GEORGE BELL AND SONS.

EXETER CATHEDRAL.—FROM THE SOUTH-WEST.

THE CATHEDRAL CHURCH OF
EXETER
A DESCRIPTION OF ITS FABRIC AND A BRIEF HISTORY OF THE EPISCOPAL SEE

BY PERCY ADDLESHAW, B.A.

LONDON GEORGE BELL & SONS 1898

CHISWICK PRESS:—CHARLES WHITTINGHAM AND CO.
TOOKS COURT, CHANCERY LANE, LONDON.

GENERAL PREFACE.

This series of monographs has been planned to supply visitors to the great English Cathedrals with accurate and well illustrated guide books at a popular price. The aim of each writer has been to produce a work compiled with sufficient knowledge and scholarship to be of value to the student of archæology and history, and yet not too technical in language for the use of an ordinary visitor or tourist.

To specify all the authorities which have been made use of in each case would be difficult and tedious in this place. But amongst the general sources of information which have been almost invariably found useful are:—firstly, the great county histories, the value of which, especially in questions of genealogy and local records, is generally recognized; secondly, the numerous papers by experts which appear from time to time in the transactions of the antiquarian and archæological societies; thirdly, the important documents made accessible in the series issued by the Master of the Rolls; fourthly, the well-known works of Britton and Willis on the English Cathedrals; and, lastly, the very excellent series of Handbooks to the Cathedrals, originated by the late Mr. John Murray, to which the reader may in most cases be referred for fuller detail, especially in reference to the histories of the respective sees.

GLEESON WHITE.
EDWARD F. STRANGE.
Editors of the Series.

AUTHOR'S PREFACE.

AMONG other books consulted the author specially owes his acknowledgments to "The Fabric Rolls"; Leland's "Itinerary"; Holler's "History"; Izacke's "Antiquities of Exeter"; Britton's "History and Antiquities of Exeter"; "Transactions of Exeter Architectural Society"; Oliver's "Lives of the Bishops of Exeter"; Murray's "Handbook of Exeter"; Canon Freeman's "Architectural History of Exeter Cathedral"; Professor Freeman's "Exeter" (Historic Towns Series); Prince's "Worthies of Devon"; Worth's "History of Devonshire"; Fuller's "Worthies of Devon"; Macaulay's "History of England"; and Green's "Short History of the English People."

P. A.

CONTENTS.

	PAGE
HISTORY OF THE CHURCH OF ST. MARY AND ST. PETER IN EXETER	1
THE FABRIC OF THE CATHEDRAL. EXTERIOR	19
The Towers	23
The West Front	24
The North Porch	31
The Roof	31
The Close	31
The Cloisters	32
The Bishop's Palace	35
THE FABRIC OF THE CATHEDRAL. INTERIOR	39
The Nave	39
The Minstrels' Gallery	43
Windows of Nave	44
Monuments in Nave	46
Monuments in the North Aisle	46
The Transepts	50
The Clock	50
The South Transept	53
The Ambulatory	58
St. Radegunde's Chapel	58
St. Edmund's Chapel	61
Sylke Chantry	61
St. Paul's Chapel	61
Chantry of the Holy Ghost	62
Chapel of St. John the Baptist	62
St. James' Chapel	62
Bishop Oldham's Chantry	65
St. Gabriel's Chapel	65
The Lady Chapel	67
Bronscombe's Tomb	67
Stafford's Tomb	67
Tomb of Sir John and Lady Doddridge	68
Tomb of Bartholomæus Iscanus	71
Tomb of Simon de Apulia	71
Tomb of Bishop Peter Quivil	71
St. Mary Magdalen Chapel	72
Speke's Chantry	72

Contents.

	PAGE
THE FABRIC OF THE CATHEDRAL. INTERIOR (*continued*).	
St. Andrew's Chapel	74
The Choir Screen	74
The Choir	78
The Choir Stalls	81
The Reredos	81
The Throne	82
The Sedilia	82
The Choir Vaulting	88
The East Window	88
TOMBS IN THE CHOIR AND CHOIR AISLES	89
THE DIOCESE OF EXETER	97
ROUGEMONT CASTLE	104
THE GUILDHALL	111

ILLUSTRATIONS.

	PAGE
Exeter Cathedral—from the South-west	*Frontispiece*
Arms of the Diocese	*Title*
Interior—Chapter House	13
Exeter Cathedral, from an old print	21
The Northern Tower	25
Portals of the West Front	29
Exeter Cathedral from the Close	35
The Bishop's Palace	37
The Nave—looking West	41
The Minstrels' Gallery	43
Brackets and Bosses	45
The Nave—looking East	47
The Transept and Clock	51
Interior of Exeter in the last century	55
Bays of Nave	59
St. James' Chapel	62
The Nave—from the South Transept	63
Screen of St. Gabriel's Chapel	66
Bishop Bronscombe's Monument	68
The Lady Chapel	69
St. George's Chapel	73
The Choir—looking West	75
Organ Screen	77
The Choir—looking East	79
The Choir before Restoration	83
The "Patterson" Pulpit	84
Sedilia in the Choir	85
Pulpit in the Choir	87
Tomb of Bishop Stapledon	90
Monument of Bishop Marshall	91
The East Gate (pulled down in 1784)	95
Old Houses in North Street	105
Rougemont Castle	108
The Guildhall, Exeter	109
PLAN OF THE CATHEDRAL	113

EXETER CATHEDRAL.

HISTORY OF THE CHURCH OF ST. MARY AND ST. PETER IN EXETER.

THE history of any ancient cathedral must always be interesting, and that of Exeter is no exception, though "it supplies less of architectural history than those churches whose whole character has been altered over and over again." A cathedral represents not only the spiritual, but the active, laborious, and artistic life of past generations. The bishop, too, was in many ways the head man of the province, and combined, not seldom, the varied qualities of priest, warrior, and statesman. The acts of such ecclesiastics were full of importance, not for their own city only, but often also for the whole nation. As men who had frequently travelled much and studied deeply, they summoned to their aid in the building and beautifying of their churches the most skilled artists and artificers of their time; so, in the story of the lives of the bishops of a diocese, the history of a cathedral's building is inextricably woven. To be elevated to a bishopric generally meant to be put into possession of great wealth—when Voysey became bishop the revenues of the see of Exeter are computed to have been £100,000 a year—and a large portion of this money was spent on works connected with the chief church of the diocese. It is not wonderful, therefore, this generosity being joined to marvellous skill and taste, that our old cathedrals are at once the despair and envy of the modern architect. And it is with a feeling of reverence that one recalls the history of those who built in the heart of each populous city "grey cliffs of lonely stone into the midst of sailing birds and silent air."

The story of Exeter has an unique interest, and its church, as we shall see, is in many respects without a rival. The fact that a building of such great beauty should adorn a city so situated is remarkable; for long after—as we read in Macaulay —weekly posts left London for various parts of England, Exeter was still, as it were, on the borders of territories scarcely explored, and was the furthest western point to which letters were conveyed from the metropolis. Fuller thus describes the county of Devonshire in his day (1646): "Devonshire hath the narrow seas on the South, the Severn on the North, Cornwall on the West, Dorset and Somersetshire on the East. A goodly province, the second in England for greatness, clear in view without measuring, as bearing a square of fifty miles. Some part thereof, as the South Hams, is so fruitful it needs no art; but generally (though not running of itself) it answers to the spur of industry. No shire showes more industrious, or so many Husbandmen, who by Marle (blew and white), Chalk, Lime, Seasand, Compost, Sopeashes, Rags and what not, make the ground both to take and keep a moderate fruitfulness; so that Virgil, if now alive, might make additions to his Georgicks, from the Plough-practice in this county. As for the natives thereof, generally they are dexterous in any employment, and Queen Elizabeth was wont to say of the gentry: *They were all born courtiers with a becomming confidence.*"

The city of Exeter is of great age. "Isca Damnoniorum, Caer Wise, Exanceaster, Exeter, keeping essentially the same name under all changes, stands distinguished as the one great city which has, in a more marked way than any other, kept its unbroken being and its unbroken position throughout all ages." But though Whitaker asserts that in the middle of the fifth century it was the seat of a bishop, Professor Freeman, with more authority, declares that the city did not become a bishop's see till the latter half of the eleventh century, at which period the bishopstools were removed from the small to the great towns. Until 703 A.D. Devonshire formed part of the vast diocese of Wessex. About the year 900 A.D. the diocese of Devon and Cornwall was divided into two—the former with its bishop's seat at Crediton—only to be reunited again a hundred and fifty years later when Leofric was appointed bishop.

The first record of a church dedicated to SS. Mary and Peter in Exeter, is that of an abbey church founded by

Athelstan. But Sweyn destroyed it seventy years later, and it seems frequently to have been attacked by invaders previous to its destruction. But in 1019 Canute endowed a new church and confirmed by charter their lands and privileges to the monks. This building must have been of some pretensions, for it was given to Leofric for his cathedral church in 1050.

With the episcopate of Leofric, Exeter first assumes the rank of a cathedral city. Under him the sees of Devon and Cornwall were once more united. Crediton, an unfortified "vill," offered plenty of chances to the Irish, Danes, and other pirates, who devastated the diocese from time to time, of successful attack. Leofric felt the urgent necessity for a change, and fixed on the walled town of Exeter to be his cathedral city. He sent a clerk to the pope asking him to write to the king recommending the change. The king readily consented, and the church of St. Mary and St. Peter was given to the bishop as his cathedral church. The event was clearly regarded as of considerable importance, for at his installation Edward the Confessor "supported his right arm and Queen Eadgytha his left." Archbishops, bishops, and nobles also assisted at the ceremony. Leofric proved a hard-working and wise prelate, and gave generously of lands and moneys to his church. He had found it but poorly furnished, the wardrobe only containing "one worthless priest's dress." He also remembered it in his will, and the great "Liber Exoniensis" was his gift.

But if the history of the see has its birth with Leofric, the story of the cathedral begins with the appointment in 1107 of Warelwast as bishop. This noteworthy man was a nephew of the Conqueror and chaplain to both William II. and Henry I. Inheriting to the full the Norman passion for building, he pulled down the Saxon edifice and began to erect a great Norman cathedral in its stead. The transeptal towers attest the magnificence of his scheme. There is nothing quite like them anywhere else, though at Barcelona and Chalons-sur-Marne may be seen something similar. But they suffice to stamp him as an architect of supreme genius. He laboured zealously in other matters, founding at Plympton a wealthy Augustinian priory; he also represented the king at Rome in his famous quarrel with Anselm. It is said that he became blind and died, an old man, at his priory of Plympton.

The next important date to notice is 1194, when Henry

Marshall, brother of Walter Earl Marshall, was made bishop. For two years the episcopal throne had remained empty, the king being absent from England in the Holy Land. But with the appointment of Marshall a most important stage is reached. King John gave to the see the tithes of the tin in Devonshire and Cornwall. This must have largely increased the episcopal income, for Marshall quickly set about completing the work Warelwast had begun a hundred years before. To this end he granted the emoluments of Lanuthinoch Church in Cornwall to be used towards defraying the cost of repairs. He also called upon each householder to show his interest in the work by subscribing, at Pentecost, an alms of "unum obolum ad minus." For the sufficient remuneration of the choral vicars he made over to them the church of St. Swithin in Woodbury, "with all its appurtenances." To Marshall we owe the Lady, Gabriel, and Magdalen chapels, also extensive additions to the nave, the north porch, and the cloister doorway. Hoker claims that "he finished the building of his church according to the Plot and foundation which his predecessors laid." But Canon Freeman[1] declared, and the above bald statement is sufficient warrant for the assertion, that "he must have done much more than this; greatly enlarging eastward upon that plan." Under his guidance the cathedral completed the Norman period of its development.

For nearly fifty years there are but scant records of work done to the building. Though Professor Freeman[2] speaks of its "not long-lived perfection," it is quite possible that Marshall's work was considered, by his own and the succeeding generation, to be final. Any interest there may be in the lives of two of the succeeding bishops, until the election of Bronscombe in 1257, is for the most part due to their labours in other matters. For example, under Simon de Apulia, the city of Exeter was divided into parishes; and by William Bruere the chapter house and stalls of the old choir were completed. He was one of the leaders of the English army at Acre in 1228. He also created the deanery of Exeter.

But with the arrival of Walter Bronscombe a new career of architectural energy begins. Now dawns that wonderful trans-

[1] "Architectural History of Exeter Cathedral," by Philip Freeman, Archdeacon and Canon of Exeter (Bell), 1888.
[2] "Exeter" (Historic Towns Series), by Professor Freeman (Longmans).

formation period, at the close of which the church stood pretty much as we now know it. Concerning Bronscombe's character there has been somewhat bitter dispute. It is certain that he was accused of craftiness and meanness. But William of Worcester, whose testimony is valuable, called him Walter le Good. Whatever may be the real truth of the matter, he seems to have made an admirable bishop, his election reflecting considerable credit on the acumen of those concerned in it. For he had not, surely, much to recommend him, at first sight, for so important a position. Though he was Archdeacon of Surrey at the time of his appointment, he was not a priest, and he was quite a young man. He was a vigorous supporter of learning throughout the diocese, probably because of his anxiety to give other men of humble origin a fair chance of making their way in the world. He restored the College of Crediton, and built one at Glaseney. He busied himself with making alterations in the cathedral church, especially caring for the restoration of the chapels of St. Mary and St. Gabriel, and the early parts of the present building are certainly his work. To his Dean and Chapter he appropriated the church of St. Bruared in Cornwall, that the feast of his patron saint, Gabriel, might be worthily maintained: "To the intent with more holy affection and more fervent zeal, even our service may not be wanting to the spirits of the heavenly court; we endeavour, according to the measure of our weakness, to bestow such honour as we are able." His tomb is preserved in the Lady Chapel.

The example given by Bronscombe was eagerly followed by Quivil, to whom belongs the credit of beginning "the fabric of St. Peter's in its new shape. He invented and designed the Decorated cathedral, and transformed the transepts. He must be classed with Warelwast as the chief of the building bishops. Admirably and sympathetically as his work was continued by those who followed him, their claim on our recognition and gratitude is less. Unfortunately, the accounts of his life are rather meagre; for one would gladly know more of a man who must have possessed architectural genius of no ordinary kind. His skill, too, seems to have been almost equalled by his generosity, for out of gratitude the Chapter promised to maintain his yearly obit. In the office of the mass, in the memento for the dead, his name was ordered to be spoken *primum et praecipium*. He seems to have given the Franciscans some cause for anger; it is suggested that his Dominican confessor urged him to treat the followers of St. Francis with severity. Anyhow, the aggrieved ones had their revenge, for the bishop's death, which happened on the eve of St. Francis, "after drinking of a certain sirrop," was popularly attributed to the direct intervention of the saint himself. He is buried in the Lady Chapel, which he had transformed and decorated with such tender care, and a slab in the centre of the pavement, bearing the legend " Petra tegit Petrum nihil officiat sibi tetrum," is dedicated to his memory.

Quivil was the first to endow the office of chaunter and Walter Secklade was the first who occupied the salaried post. So says Prince in his "Worthies of Devon," and probably he is accurate. A very pretty quarrel that had long agitated the antiquaries was thus settled. For it was contended by some that John the chaunter was the first to hold the office, by others that Quivil founded the office and that the bishop's name was really John Cauntor. But Prince's explanation that the office was only endowed by Quivil and that it existed before his day was entirely satisfactory, we may hope, to the supporters of the rival theories. The above-mentioned Walter Secklade was murdered "about two in the morning" on his return from matins in the cathedral cloisters. The murderers escaped through the south gate of the city, which was left open. An extraordinary sensation was created, not in Exeter only but throughout England. The bishop invited Edward I. and his queen to keep their Christmas at the Palace. We are told "they were very industrious in finding out the murtherers." At last Alfred Dupont, an ex-mayor and porter of the south gate, was found guilty and executed accordingly. Perhaps, had the office of chaunter not been endowed, Walter Secklade might have continued for many long years to chaunt in sonorous voice "matins, vespers, obits, and the like." At any rate the story is worth telling, being an interesting picture of manners in the middle ages. One only regrets the details are so scanty. They should be remarkable indeed since they caused a king to play the policeman.

Quivil's successor was Thomas de Bytton, Dean of Wells. Under his guidance the work of transformation planned by his predecessor was loyally continued, the original design being faithfully adhered to. Though Bytton appears to have been less active outside his diocese than many of the Exeter bishops, his mode of life must have commended itself to a large circle. A grant of forty days' indulgence was the reward of all those who availed themselves of his spiritual ministrations, or offered prayers for his prosperity during his life and after death. Among the signatures appended to the document notifying this singular privilege are those of numerous archbishops and bishops, among them being those of the archbishops of Cosensa and Jerusalem, and Manfred, Bishop of St. Mark's, Venice. "The seal of Manfred," Dr. Oliver says, "is perfect; he stands robed, with a piece of embroidery on his alb. The crozier is simply curved. His legend is S. MANFREDI. DEI. GRA. EPISCOP. SCI. MARCHI." It was dated at Rome in the year 1300. Possibly Bytton's great learning, by which he had risen to be Professor of Canon Law at Oxford and Pope's Chaplain, was partly the reason of so notable a compliment. But the great work he was doing in the cathedral church of his diocese, we may hope, had not a little to do with the honour. For to him we owe the entire transformation of the choir with its aisles. Bytton's labours were, indeed, very great. We hear of large quantities of stone procured from Barley, and of sandstone from Salcombe and Branscombe. He also put a good deal of stained glass into the windows; so that in the eleventh year of his episcopate the following item is recorded: "Master Walter le Verrouer for setting the glass of the upper gable and of eight upper windows, and of six windows in the aisles of the new work, in gross, £4 10s." Bytton was succeeded, in 1308, by Walter de Stapledon, the most famous of all the bishops of Exeter. A younger son of Sir Richard Stapledon of Annery, his appointment was the first of a succession of aristocratic nominations. He, too, had been a professor of canon law at Oxford, was a chaplain to the Pope and precentor of the cathedral in the university. The feast given after his enthronement was unusually splendid, the revenues for a whole year being spent on the festivities. It seems as though, conscious of his great talents, he determined to signalize his accession to the episcopal office by some event of unusual magnificence. It must be remembered that Exeter was at this time one of the largest and richest sees in England. As Professor Freeman has pointed out, "The Bishop of Exeter, like the Archbishop of York, was the spiritual head of a separate people." Stapledon set about expediting the work of transforming the cathedral into the Decorated style in vigorous fashion. The Fabric Rolls record that he himself gave the (then) enormous sum of £1,800 towards defraying the cost. His generosity encouraged others to subscribe liberally towards the building fund. One of his first duties was to complete the choir, a payment being made to William Canon of £35 2s. 8d. for "marble from Corfe for the columns." But the choir was really Bytton's, the new bishop had only to give to it "a few final, though not unimportant, touches." But he found plenty of work to hand that might receive the impress of his sole initiative. He designed and completed the triforium arcade above the choir arches, and directed the colouring of the choir vault, the total expenses for oil and colour being estimated at £1 9s. 7¾d. By these "final touches" the transformation of the choir into the Decorated style was completed. But Stapledon determined to further enrich his already beautiful church with accessories of surpassing splendour. He erected a high altar of silver, also the beautiful sedilia, and though there has been a good deal of dispute about the matter, the more trustworthy authorities attribute to him the bishop's throne of carved wood. At any rate, in 1312, there is a charge of £6 12s. 8½d. for "timber for the bishop's seat." The altar, unfortunately, has disappeared, but it is reputed to have cost a sum equivalent to £7,000 of our money. Canon Freeman thus describes it: "Above, as it should seem (for the entries are very obscure), was a canopy of considerable extent, wrought with bosses internally. The whole seems to have been surmounted by a figure of our Lord."

With Stapledon building seems to have been a favourite recreation: for though he gave most largely both of time and money to the cathedral work, he found opportunity to build and endow Harts Hall, Stapledon Inn—now Exeter College—Oxford, and the "very fair" Essex House in London. In 1320 he was created Lord High Treasurer by Edward II., and later in the same year received from his sovereign the power of holding pleas of "hue and cry" in the lands, tenements, and fees of the bishopric in the county of Cornwall. The neglected condition of many of the parish churches in his diocese distressed him, and almost his last public appearance in the west of England was at Lawhitton, where he spoke severely on this matter to his Dean and Chapter, and bade them see to

it that in future there should be no good cause of complaint.
In the autumn of 1324 he set out for France, accompanying
the young Prince Edward, who was about to do homage to the
French king for the duchies of Aquitaine and Poitou. But his
"irreproachable integrity" made him unpopular, and his life
was threatened. On his return to England he saw that a crisis
was at hand, and almost immediately after his arrival Queen
Eleanor landed on the coast of Suffolk. Edward II., in a brief
moment of wisdom, assigned to the faithful bishop the government of London and retreated to Bristol. But it was too late
to effect a reconciliation or prevent a catastrophe. With a firm
hand Stapledon endeavoured to restore order and quiet, and
promulgated a decree by which all rebels were excommunicated.
But the citizens, wisely perhaps, sided with the conquerors,
and the bishop died a martyr to duty. The story is well told
in the French chronicles quoted by Dr. Oliver. "The Bishop
of Exeter, riding towards his inn or hotel, in Eldeanes-lane
for dinner, encountered the mob, and, hearing them shout
Traitor, he rode rapidly to St. Paul's for sanctuary, but was
unhorsed, taken to Cheapside, stripped and beheaded. About
the hours of vespers, the same day, October 15th, the choir of
St. Paul's took up the headless body of the prelate and
conveyed it to St. Paul's, but, on being informed that he died
under sentence, the body was brought to St. Clement's beyond
the Temple, but was ejected; so that the naked corpse, with a
rag given by the charity of a woman, was laid on the spot
called 'Le Lawles Cherche,' and without any grave, lay there
with those of his two esquires, without office of priest or clerk.
His house was attacked, the gates burned, quantities of jewels
and plate plundered."

In another account of his death it is stated that his head
was "fixed on a long pole by way of trophy, that it might be
to all beholders a lasting memorial of his attempted crime."
There was a personal reason why the bishop was unpopular
among the citizens, for "he procured that the justices in eyre
should sit in London; on which occasion, because the citizens
had committed various offences, they were heavily punished
by the loss of their liberties, by pecuniary mulcts, and by
bodily chastisment, as they deserved." But the queen caused
his body to be rescued from the "hepe of rubische," and it was
removed to Exeter, where it lies on the north side of the choir.

He left behind him large sums of money and plate, a valuable library and, unique item, ninety-one rings. He was certainly one of the greatest prelates in English history, and though he may have been, as his detractors asserted, "finnische and without pite," he was revered in his diocese, and left an example of courage and honesty to succeeding generations. His executors, animated by a wish to do what he would have desired, distributed £210 8s. 8d. in charities, and gave considerable sums to other worthy objects. And the Abbot of Hartland caused the 15th of October to be solemnly observed, out of gratitude for the late bishop's bounty, and decreed that on that day "for all future times 'XIII. pauperes in aulâ abbatis, pro ipsius anima, pascantur.'"

To follow so redoubtable a prelate as Stapledon must have been an extremely difficult task. But Grandisson, who was appointed after Birkley's short episcopate ended, has sometimes been called the most magnificent prelate who ever filled the see. He was nominated directly by the pope, and consecrated by his holiness at Avignon. His chief glory is that he allowed the splendour of the see in no wise to diminish, and he kept up the Stapledon traditions of princely hospitality and well-doing. His reputation of "grave, wise, and politick" seems to have been fairly earned. As a descendant of the great ducal house of Burgundy, he had lived much with princes and held the position of nuncio "at the courts of all the mightiest princes of Christendom." His election was carried out in direct opposition to the wishes of the canons of Exeter, but a wise choice had been made, and by his long episcopate of forty years he gained honour for himself and good fortune for his people. He had to face many difficulties at first that might well have appalled a weaker man. The tragic death of Stapledon had terrified all men, the great work of that giant intellect remained unfinished, and required some one of exceptional energy to complete it fitly. Added to these difficulties, the episcopal manors had been plundered and the accounts were terribly muddled. Grandisson, luckily, was a man who looked upon difficulties as things to be overcome. He applied to the members of his family for funds, and the negotiations are interesting, for the borrower is the only person who maintained his dignity unimpaired. With courteous pertinacity and a fitting show of priestly anger, he finally got the supplies he needed. With indomitable energy he managed to arrange in perfect order the confused affairs of his diocese. Turning eagerly to the task of completing the building of his church, he transformed the six west bays of the nave, vaulting, aisles, west window, and north cloister. In spiritual and temporal affairs he was equally busy. Twice at least he was the host of royalty, once the Black Prince visited his diocese with the captive king of France. The same illustrious warrior, shortly before his death, again enjoyed the bishop's hospitality.

In 1343 Grandisson was sent as ambassador to Rome, and the sound sense he had shown at Exeter was equally apparent in the conduct of his mission, so that it was written of him that "he did his message with much wisdom and honour." Certainly, few bishops have had so exalted a view of the dignity and importance of the episcopal office, and none ever dared to fight more boldly for his imagined rights. When the Archbishop Mepham determined to make a personal visitation, Grandisson's anger was kindled. Gathering round him a body of armed retainers, he met the archbishop at the west door of the cathedral. There might have been a bloody conflict, for neither prelate was likely to give way. Fortunately, wiser counsels prevailed, and the quarrel was referred to the pope. His holiness decided in Grandisson's favour, and "the dispute did half break Mepham's heart, and the Pope, siding with the Bishop of Exeter, did break the other half." So writes Fuller, and the quaint sentence does not lack authority, for the archbishop died shortly after the termination of the quarrel.

Grandisson remembered his cathedral in his will. He bequeathed to his successors his crozier and mitre, and to the diocese 2,000 marks. At his funeral, in accordance with his instructions, a hundred poor persons were clothed and money was distributed among the prisoners and the sick. He remembered, too, the needs of the poorer clergy and the hospitals, while to Pope Urban and Edward III. he left splendid legacies. His funeral, as his life, was simple and economical. For his magnificent presents, his gorgeous works on the structure of his church, were made possible by his own simple, almost parsimonious manner of living. He was buried in the chapel of St. Radegunde, but the tomb was destroyed in Elizabeth's time, and his ashes lie "no man knows where."

Brantyngham, the next bishop, completed the cloisters, the

east window and west front. But, as Canon Freeman has said, "the rest of the works of this and the following century are little else than petty restorations; of course in a later and inferior style, and generally to the detriment of the building." But there is still much in the history of the church and the see that deserves a passing notice. Under Brantyngham, the old feud that Grandisson had finished so satisfactorily to himself, began again. But the victory this time was with the archbishop. At Topsham, a village not far from the city, the bishop's servants attacked savagely the archbishop's mandatory. Full of zeal for the honour, as they conceived it, of their own prelate, they made the wretched creature eat the archbishop's writ and seal. But the meal of parchment and wax did not by any means settle the dispute. The bishop's cause, indeed, was irretrievably damaged, the king was furious, an appeal to the pope was unsuccessful, and Brantyngham had to make full submission to the offended primate. Henceforth the archbishop's right of visitation was not opposed. Had another than Grandisson been bishop in Mepham's day the dispute would never, probably, have arisen; for the archbishop was undoubtedly only exercising his rights, such visitations being according to canon, and of ancient usage.

The next bishop whose episcopate is important is Lacey, who glazed the nave windows and raised the chapter house. He has, too, an unique claim on our regard because of his saintly character. As yet no saint had made the cathedral venerable and the sentimental affection and profit which saintly relics were wont to cause was still lacking. It is said that Iscanius had contrived to get some relics of Becket for his cathedral, but there was no local saint, and this want Lacey supplied. Yet the days of his episcopacy were by no means absolutely calm. At the very moment of his accession he involved himself in a dispute with the city corporation as to the liberties of his cathedral. Nor was he, though meek and holy, at all inclined to submit to any infringement of his prerogatives, even when the transgressor happened to wear a crown. Indeed, he most successfully protested against the conduct of Henry VI., who held a jail delivery in the bishop's hall. Two men were condemned to death, but the bishop remonstrated so forcibly against this exercise of temporal authority within the precincts of the sanctuary, that they were released. As an author Lacey

History of the Church. 13

gained a considerable reputation. His "Liber Pontificalis" is still preserved, his office in honour of Raphael the Archangel

THE CHAPTER HOUSE (FROM BRITTON'S "EXETER," 1826).

was admired and used in many cathedrals and churches. When he died miracles were performed at his tomb, and pilgrimages were constantly made to it by the common people.

It is not surprising that from this time onward the architectural history of the cathedral becomes less important. Four great periods were past, and the fifth was nearing its end. Under Warelwast and Marshall the old Saxon cathedral had given way to the Norman; which was superseded in its turn by the Early English work of Bruere and Bronscombe. Then with Quivil came the fourth period, and the complete transformation of the building into the Decorated style. The fifth and last change is the introduction of Perpendicular work, chiefly noticeable in the upper portion of the chapter house and the great west screen. The day of the great builders was waning fast. The old faith that inspired them was dwindling, the attraction of national concerns was too great for local effort. Moreover, the desire to make intricately beautiful, right enough in itself, had vitiated, as it was bound to do, the taste of architect and builder. The old Norman cathedrals, however rugged, were imposing in their stern and simple strength. The desire for decoration affected various transformations, which at first left the building more beautiful and not less strong. But gradually the simplicity and strength disappear altogether. Luckily, as we shall see, the great church of St. Mary and St. Peter has suffered less than most buildings that have undergone so many changes. "As it is, the church of Exeter is a remarkable case of one general design being carried out through more than a hundred years." The church is Quivil's design, and the variations, though important, do not seriously detract from it.

The events of the next five hundred years belong more to the history of the see, and even of England, than to the church. In the election of George Neville (1458) we notice the immense value put on noble birth. Only one other reason can be alleged as weighing with those responsible for the choice. And this reason is so ridiculous as to be almost incredible. None the less it had, doubtless, a good deal to do with Neville's election to the bishopric. He was not only a brother to the great Earl of Warwick, but he early showed his intention of keeping up the almost kingly traditions of his family. Here is an account of the festivities that took place at Oxford after he had performed "his exercises in the nave of St. Mary's Church, as the custom now is, and before was, for nobleman's sons." "Such entertainment was given for two days space that the memory of man being not now able to produce, I have thought it worth my pains to remember. On the first day therefore were 600 messes of meat, and on the second 300 for the entertainment only of scholars and certain of the Proceeders, relations and acquaintances." A later Oxford historian asserts that Neville was elected chancellor the very next year "by an appreciative university!" It is not at all unlikely, therefore, that this display of hospitality had something to do with his being chosen bishop, as being a fitting successor to such prelates as Grandisson. For four years after his election he was unable, owing to his youth, to be consecrated. But by one of those ecclesiastical scandals, which seem not to have annoyed or astonished his contemporaries, he was permitted to enjoy the temporalities of the see. At the age of twenty-seven he was fully ordained bishop, and a few years later was transferred to York. During the episcopate of his successor, Bothe, the city was besieged by Perkin Warbeck. In 1478 he was translated to Bath and Wells, and, inspired by a dream, caused the building of the abbey church in the former city.

From 1504 to 1519 Oldham, a Lancashire man, was bishop. He built the Oldham and Speke chapels.

Voysey, who succeeded him, lived during the reign of Henry VIII. His courtly manners made him popular. In addition to his rich ecclesiastical office, he became Lord President of Wales and tutor to the Princess Mary. He founded the town of Sutton Coleshill, now Sutton Coldfield, and introduced there the making of kersies. On this enterprise he spent the larger part of his fortune. At the accession of Edward VI. he was left undisturbed, though suspected of favouring the old religion. But when a rising in favour of the unreformed church disturbed the western counties, he was accused of participation in the movement, and resigned his charge. But he retained the temporalities, and on Mary's accession was reinstated. But he was nearly 103 years old, and soon after died at his town of Sutton Coleshill in 1555.

Miles Coverdale, the translator, with Tyndale, of the Bible, his successor, was bishop for only two years. He was unpopular, although his life was "most godly" and virtuous. But "the common people," says Hoker, "whose bottles would receive no new wine, could not brook or digest him, for no other cause but because he was a preacher of the Gospel, an enemy to Papistry, and a married man." This dislike is easily accounted for. Exeter was very far from London, the new ideas travelled slowly, and the west was staunchly conservative. As with many reformers, too, his zeal was spoilt by indiscretion; the sternness of the Puritan militated against his success, and people preferred the old errors more becomingly supported. His successor, Turberville, was a man more after the heart of the people, and he won praise from Protestant and Catholic alike.

He was succeeded by William Alleyn, and an interesting commentary on Voysey's extravagance is to be noticed. By royal charter the number of canons was limited to nine.

In 1627 the see was held by Joseph Hall, a man of great distinction. Though too conciliatory to care greatly for Laud's policy, he wrote a justly famous "Defence of the Church of England and her doctrines." After his translation to Norwich he underwent a good deal of persecution, which he himself has recorded, and was for six months a prisoner in the Tower. He is buried in Higham parish church, his monument a skeleton holding "in the right hand a bond to death sealed and signed, 'Debemus morti nos nostrique,' and in his left the same bond torn and cancelled, with the endorsement 'Persolvit et quietus est.'" Fuller says of the famous satirist that he was "not unhappy at controversies, more happy at comments, very good in his characters, better in his sermons, best of all in his meditations."

John Gauden, who became bishop in 1660, was far more fortunate, though probably not more happy. He does not seem to have been over scrupulous, and his desire for "a good manger" is unpleasantly obvious. But as the author of the EIKΩN BAΣIΛIKH he is remembered. The authorship has been disputed, but Charles II. certainly recognized his claim, and Clarendon believed his assertions about it. He was clever enough to have written even a better book, and there is no sufficient ground for depriving him of the honour. It is certain that he owed his preferment to his reputed merit as its author; though, oddly enough, he had taken the covenant and preached a notorious sermon against "pictures, images, and other superstitions of popery." But he publicly recanted, later, and protested against the murder of the king, whose supposed last prayers and meditations he was skilfully inventing. After being in Exeter two years he was removed to Worcester. But he had looked to become bishop of Winchester, and it is said that his death was hastened by disappointment.

Seth Ward, who followed him, had, as dean of Exeter, distinguished himself by his zeal and courage. He drove from the cathedral precincts the buyers and sellers who had encroached thereon, and the partition wall that divided the cathedral was taken down at his request. During the Commonwealth "the building which was now formally called 'the late cathedral church' was divided by a brick wall into two places of worship, known as East Peter's and West Peter's." The east portion was used by the Independents and the west by Presbyterians. Ward spent £20,000 on redeeming the cathedral from the degradation it had suffered, and bought an organ, "esteemed the best in England," which cost him £2,000. He was translated to Salisbury in 1687. He was a man of considerable ability and was a founder of the Royal Society.

Sparrow succeeded to the see in 1667. During his episcopate the Grand Duke Cosmo visited Exeter and wondered at the worthy bishop, his wife, and his nine children. The Duke of Tuscany was spoken of in the local reports as the Duke of Tuskey, and he received from the corporation a gift of "£20, or thereabouts." Sparrow, on his translation to Norwich, was succeeded by Lamplough, whose political acumen, at any rate, compels admiration, if not respect. He fervently bade his flock rally round the unfortunate James II., and then, posting to London, was rewarded by the grateful king with the archbishopric of York. He then without any compunction crowned William of Orange, King of England. But his smartness availed little, "for within three years continuance of that high throne of York he was summoned before an higher." Macaulay has finely described the entrance of the prince into the cathedral. "As he passed under the gorgeous screen, that renowned organ, scarcely surpassed by any of those which are the boast of his native Holland, gave out a peal of triumph. He mounted the bishop's seat, a stately throne, rich with the carving of the fifteenth century. Burnet stood below, and a crowd of warriors and nobles appeared on the right hand and on the left. The singers robed in white sang the 'Te Deum.' When the chaunt was over Burnet read the Prince's declaration; but as soon as the first words were uttered, prebendaries and singers crowded

C

in all haste out of the choir. At the close, Burnet, in a loud voice, cried, 'God save the Prince of Orange,' and many fervent voices answered 'Amen.'" This is certainly the most remarkable, as it is also the last, of the great historical events that have happened under the shadow of the cathedral walls. There had been nothing to compare with it since the day when Grandisson with his armed retainers met Mepham at the west front three hundred years before. Offspring Blackall is the last bishop we need mention. He was a famous preacher, and worked hard for the comfort and education of the indigent classes. To him Exeter owes her charity schools.

Of the remaining bishops there is nothing of moment to record.

It has seemed wiser in this brief sketch to devote a paragraph to each of those bishops who either architecturally or historically made their episcopates events of national importance. The early bishops especially busied themselves exceedingly in making beautiful their principal church. It is by knowing something of their lives and times that one can best appreciate their labours, and trace with intelligent interest the causes of the splendid result to be studied minutely in the remaining chapters of this book.

Moreover, all lovers of the great in art, all who love what is beautiful, as all may with a little trouble, will not be sorry to have even a passing acquaintance with those who have wrought so nobly. And this short notice of the most famous of the bishops of Exeter proves that they were for the most part chosen, not for their lineage, however splendid, nor the favour they had gained as gracious courtiers, but for their excellent lives, their plain living and high thinking, their taste and learning, and for qualities which, if rarer now, were not common even hundreds of years ago.

THE FABRIC OF THE CATHEDRAL.

THE EXTERIOR.

BEFORE examining the various details, it may be well to recall the following facts, which have already been referred to. First, the cathedral was Saxon and remained so for nearly seventy years; then came a Norman bishop who pulled down the existing building and replaced it by the foundations and towers of a finer one. For ninety-nine years, sometimes languishingly, sometimes vigorously, the work continued: so that by the end of Marshall's episcopate (1206) Warelwast's noble ambition was realized. Between this date and 1280 the church was scarcely touched, but a chapter house was built by Bishop Bruere "to God and the Church of St. Mary and St. Peter, a sufficient area to make a Chapter House in our garden near the Tower of St. John." A third style, Early English, was then introduced, to be followed by the almost complete transformation of the entire building into the Decorated style. Following on this we get some examples of Perpendicular work. Now, this series of changes is not only noticeable in itself, but because it has not affected the building in a way that might have been expected. The first impression, indeed, that a view of the exterior gives one, is that it is the result of one design, which is largely the case. It is only on closer inspection that the remnants of the pre-decorated periods are visible. "The Church," as Professor Freeman neatly puts it, "grew up after one general pattern, but with a certain advance in detail as the work went westward."

The second thing that strikes the visitor is that he has never seen a church quite like it. "It forms a class by itself, and can be compared with nothing save its own miniature at Ottery."

Putting aside the Saxon cathedral of Leofric it is possible to trace four distinct styles in what has been wisely called "the noblest monument of religious zeal of our forefathers in the

west of England." But in discovering these the feeling of
wonder increases as the building is found to be not a mere
jumble but a complete whole. Though it is possible to date
the separate parts of the edifice, and recognize the varying
forms of workmanship, the architects laboured with so clear an
understanding of a beautiful result to be attained, that there is
no appearance of patchwork.

The best views of the building are those to be got from a
distance. In some ways this is not without compensation ;
for the cathedral church was, and is, not only splendid as a
building, but the centre of the spiritual life of the diocese. It
is, therefore, appropriate that it should seem most beautiful to
the dwellers in the villages and hamlets beyond the city, giving
them, as it were, a kind of property in the building, which they
might not have felt had it been less visible. Nearing Exeter
by train, from the Plymouth side, the noble roof and towers are
seen above the red houses of the city. The site, indeed, was
well chosen. Below the hill on which the city stands are
gardens gay with flowers and fair apple orchards. Above, there
is a blue sky richer and deeper than is usual in England. On all
sides but one stretches the beautiful Devonshire country, meadow,
hedgerow, and wooded hill. On that side the Exe flows
rapidly, broadening as it goes, towards the sea. Southward but
a few miles, the blue channel waters creep up against the yellow
sand dunes. No cathedral, not even Lincoln, boasts a more lovely
and appropriate position. "In the minds of all early Christians,"
says Mr. Ruskin, "the church itself was most frequently symbo-
lized under the image of a ship." There is no country so
saturated with traditions of the sea as Cornwall and Devon.
"Exe terra"—out of the earth—is sometimes declared to be
the derivation of the name Exeter. But it was probably only
the grateful jest of some seaman who found himself, after the
winter storms, gliding up the quiet river with the city walls
rising up before him. But the remembrance of such western
heroes as Raleigh and Drake, who bade their followers sit well
in order, and strike—

> "The sounding furrows, for my purpose holds
> To sail beyond the sunset and the baths
> Of all the Western stars until I die," [1]

[1] Tennyson's "Ulysses."

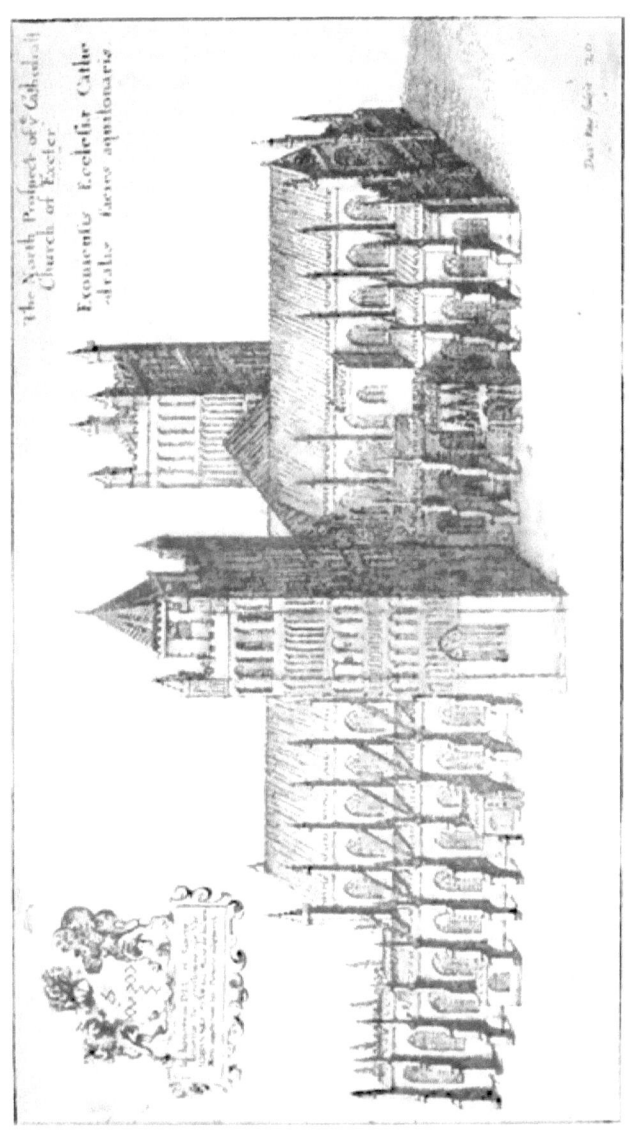

EXETER CATHEDRAL, FROM AN OLD PRINT.

makes one realize how fit it is that the towers of the cathedral should look across the country to the "deep waters," and be to the mariner as the masts of a vessel whereon was safety, however fierce the storm.

From many parts of the surrounding country fine views may be obtained, from Waddlesdown, Alphington Causeway, and many a canal and river bank.

A closer view is, at first, most disappointing. Every writer has echoed Dr. Oliver's regret that it should be surrounded "by dwelling-houses of such disparate character." But even a nearer survey is, with patience, rewarded. The towers, exquisitely traceried windows, sculptured doorways, and titanic roof, easily persuade us to forget its mean surroundings. From the palace grounds the best near view is obtainable; and by the courtesy of the bishop, admission is readily granted to visitors.

The Towers.—To many these will be the most interesting portion of the building. The exterior of no other cathedral boasts so unique a feature. Their position is extraordinary and has given rise to endless controversies. It has been suggested that they were meant to stand as western towers, and that the building was to stand east of them, and that, as an afterthought, they were converted into transepts. But Canon Freeman, the great authority on the cathedral, dismisses this view as merely attractive. They would certainly be more elaborate, he thinks, if they had been built as western towers, but they have neither portal nor ornamental work. Indeed, up to more than half their height they have very much the appearance of fortresses. It may well be that they served as such in Stephen's time, for the northern one was severely battered. It differs somewhat in detail from that on the south side, there being an interlacing arcade half-way up, possibly being rebuilt so when the devastation caused by the siege was being repaired. There are six stages on each tower, but only the four top ones are in any way ornamented. These have blind arcades and window openings of circular form; but the details differ slightly on each. On the summit of each, at the four angles, are square turrets. Bishop Courtenay altered the north tower in order that it might receive the great bell from Llandaff, the sixth stage now being Perpendicular. But the south tower, which happily was neither battered, nor partially demolished for more peaceful reasons, is to this day Norman throughout. The effect of these transeptal towers is so fine as to make us regret their rarity. As Canon Freeman finely says, "our twofold towers well image forth that ancient gesture of prayer which prevailed alike among Pagans and Israelites, the lifting up of the outspread palms to heaven." But there are most practical reasons, also, in their favour, and a consideration of them tends to increase one's wonder that they should not be found more frequently. In the first place it is possible to get a continuous, uniform, stretch of vault, the roof being broken by no central tower. Also the plan is more symmetrical, aisle tallies with aisle, chapel with chapel. Again, by building transeptal towers and discarding the usual central tower, the interior escapes a danger it is often hard to overcome, the difficulty of holding up the central tower. It is quite possible that Warelwast was far-seeing enough to anticipate this trouble. The histories of other cathedrals prove it to be a very real one. In 1107 the tower of Winchester fell in. At Salisbury the spire is still a constant source of anxiety, despite "a complex arrangement of iron bands and ties," which has been reinforced more than once. The tower of Chichester collapsed in 1861. There is a legend of the fall of a central tower at Christchurch Priory, and many other instances could be found, such as Norwich, Selby, Peterborough, and Wells.

Originally these two towers were cut off, by two arches underneath, from the body of the church. But Quivil, wishing to enlarge the interior, did so by "throwing the Tower spaces into it."

The West Front.—This is very foreign in appearance, reminding one of many French cathedrals. It is the least effective part of the building, though containing details of great beauty. It consists of three storeys. The part above the screen is the work of Grandisson, and must have been finished before 1369. Doubtless, his object in beginning his work at the west end was that he might be buried in the restored chapel of St. Radegunde. This desire of the bishops of old to prepare for themselves a place of burial is curious and common. The lowest and most protruding portion is the screen; receding somewhat, the second stage is the west wall of the nave, pierced by a decorated Gothic window of very remarkable beauty. Above this, receding still further, is a gable containing a smaller window of triangular form. In the niche

The Photochrom Co Photo.

THE NORTHERN TOWER.

above stands the statue of St. Peter, the patron saint of the cathedral. The general result, though elaborate, is heavy and not quite pleasing. The building is low, and the ornate and intricate arrangement still further reduces the height. The buttresses of solid masonry that counteract the thrust of the nave arcades contribute still more to this unsatisfactory result. The sloping walls, embattled and flanked by embattled turrets on each side of the nave, conceal both the nave aisles and the buttresses of the nave aisles; nor does the rich decoration afford any compensation for so unusual an arrangement.

Still, the screen remains the most noticeable feature of the west front. It contains a mass of figures representing angels, warriors, kings, and saints. There are three rows of these. The lowest row consists of angelic figures each sustaining a triple pilaster with capitals. On these capitals stand the statues of the second row, a long line of knights and kings, above which are the angels and apostles of the third row. Above the third row stand two figures, said to represent Athelstan and Edward the Confessor. The former once drove out the Britons from the city, the latter, as we know, founded the bishopric. The screen is Brantyngham's work, and the armour and crowns worn by the heroes and kings is of the time of Richard II. The choice of personages to be honoured seems to have been unlimited. Six of the kings of Wessex are placed on the top row among statues of the evangelists, Noah, Deborah, Gideon, but the reason for their introduction into such high company is not easy to discover. According to the Davy MS., the thirty-five figures of the upper row, beginning at the south, represent:

Ina	1	St. Simon	13
Caedwalla	2	St. James the Less	14
Kentwaed | Kings of	3	St. Thomas	15
Kenwaeck | Wessex	4	St. James	16
Cwichrem	5	St. John	17
Kenglis	6	St. Paul	18
St. Boniface	7	King Athelstan	19
St. Birinus	8	King Richard II.	20
King Ethelbert	9	St. Peter	21
St. Augustine	10	St. Andrew	22
St. Mark	11	St. Philip	23
St. Luke	12	St. Matthias	24

St. Bartholomew	. 25	Barak . .		31
St. Jude . . .	. 26	Gideon .		32
St. John . . .	. 27	Jephthah .		33
St. Matthew . .	. . 28	Samson .		34
Noah	. . 29	Samuel .		35
Deborah . . .	. 30			

In the lower row, beginning on the north, immediately under the figure of Samuel:

Canute	1	William II	17
Edgar	2	A king with a dog .	18
Ethelred	3	Two bishops . . . 19,	20
Justice } Above the	4	John	21
Fortitude } northern	5	Edward	22
Discipline } door	6	Edward III. } Over	23
Edward II. . .	7	Black Prince } southern	24
Henry III. .	8	} door	
Two bishops	9, 10	Godfrey de Bouillon, with	
Richard I. . . .	11	hawk on wrist . . .	25
Henry II. . . .	12	Stephen, Count of Blois .	26
Stephen . . .	13	Guy de Lusignan . . .	27
Henry I. . . .	14	Ethelwold	28
William I. . . .	15	Alfred	29
Robert of Normandy .	16	Edward the elder .	30

The statues of James the Less and William I. are very successful modern imitations of the older statues, and are the work of Stevens.

Possibly the real success the sculptors achieved in some of these figures is due to the generous choice of subject allowed to them. But though, when looked at piecemeal, it is impossible not to admire "the remarkable, characteristic and beautiful sculpture," one is compelled to regret that there is so much of it. The crowding together of so large a number of figures does greatly destroy the effect each might have made on its individual merits. Above the screen is a platform, from which the bishop probably blessed the people and the minstrels welcomed with song the approach of royal or illustrious visitors.

The three doorways in the screen are worthy of notice, being richly decorated. That on the south side is the most beautiful,

PORTALS OF WEST FRONT.

and contains two fine pieces of sculpture, one generally declared to be an angel appearing to Joseph in a dream, the other certainly recording the Adoration of the Shepherds. The central porch is decorated with sculptured foliage, and the Crucifixion is exhibited on the central boss of the groined roof tracery.

The North Porch.—This is part of Grandisson's work, and is of rare beauty. The roof is vaulted, on the central boss of which is a finely-carved Agnus Dei. Within a recess of the eastern wall are three headless figures, representing, in the centre, the Crucifixion, St. Mary and St. John standing on either side. Over the inside doorway is a niche that probably once held a figure of the Virgin.

The Roof.—It has been contended that the unbroken stretch of leaden roof is too much exposed, and helps to dwarf the appearance of the building. But to many it will seem one of the most striking, as it certainly is one of the most unique, features of the church. The cresting of the roof in a delicate fleur-de-lis pattern is most effective, and does much to refute the above-quoted opinion.

The Close.—This was an important adjunct to all cathedrals in the days following the Conquest. We have seen that on one occasion at least the Cathedral Church of Exeter was severely bombarded, with the result that the northern tower differs considerably from the southern in places. The church, then, we may presume, was intended to be used, when necessary, as a fortress; but as it was also something else very different, this necessity was rather shunned than courted. Therefore it was customary to separate the church from the world by walls and gates of proved strength. This space so secured formed an outer fortress, against which the attacks of an enemy must, perforce, have been directed first. It placed entirely in the hands of the clergy the defence of their own church, a task they were quite capable of performing with credit; for Matthew Paris tells us of one bishop of Exeter, Bruere, that he displayed activity both "spiritual and temporal" in the Holy Land. The defence of the city, that of the sacred building being thus provided for, was the business of the captains and men-at-arms. The walls and gates of the close have vanished, without leaving a trace of their existence. One privilege, however, yet haunts the place—the corporation have no jurisdiction over it.

The Cloisters.—Canon Freeman thinks that originally the cloister " was confined to the east side, as a necessary communication between the chapter house and the great south door of the nave." During Stapledon's time a desire had been evinced to enlarge this cloister; and in 1323 there is a record to the effect that eight heads had been carved for vaulting the cloister. In the Fabric Rolls are entries that show the work of building proceeded with some activity and considerable cheapness. Here are a few extracts that are interesting:

" Twenty-five horse-loads of sand for the cloister, 9d. A thousand lath nails and healing pins for do. S. Clifford sculpanti 18 capites 3-9 : 10 do. 2 -."

By 1342 the work was probably finished to the north, and forty years later the whole must have been completed. It has been said that the old cloisters were inferior to those of Worcester and Gloucester. But they must have had considerable merit if Mr. Pearson's restoration really represents, and there is little doubt it does, the old structure.

It is curious that the cloisters, certainly the least offensive and not the most beautiful part of the cathedral, should have suffered so severely at the hands of the Puritans. For on the whole the cathedral proper escaped with but small damage. Professor Freeman, in discussing the alleged desecrations suffered by St. Mary and St. Peter, after the entrance of Fairfax and his army into the city, writes thus : " The account in Mercurius Rusticus, which has given vogue to the common story is wholly untrue." He further adds : " Some fanatic soldier may, indeed, according to the story, have broken off the head of Queen Elizabeth, mistaking her for our Lady. But no general mutilation or desecration took place at this time. And at Exeter, one form of mutilation, which specially affected the west front, was not the work of enemies but of devotees. For ages the country folk who came into the city loved to carry home a " Peter stone for the healing of their ailments." It is only fair to add that Canon Freeman refers in very different language to the result of the occupation by the Puritan, and certainly, as far as the cloisters are concerned, we may believe that they suffered from their fanaticism until we have a more certain date given for their destruction. It should be noted, however, that in the fifteenth century the Dean and Chapter bitterly complained of the conduct of the Exeter boys, who-

EXETER CATHEDRAL. FROM THE CLOSE.

played "unlawfull games as the toppe, queke, penny pryke & most atte tenys" in the cloisters, whereby they were "defowled & the glas windows all to-brost." But at this time the cathedral and municipal authorities were far from friendly to each other. Dr. Oliver writes of them in his day that they "have disappeared with the exception of part of a fluted column at the west corner of the carpenter's shop." With the debris small and mean houses were built. On the 30th of October, 1657, we are given a hint as to what may have been the meaning of this wanton destruction. Apparently the ground set apart for "the convenience of the studious and contemplative" was found to have valuable attributes as a market-place, for on the above day the "Friday cloth market for serges and other drapery" was ordered to be held in this place. Commerce did not triumph for long, though, as only three years later the buyers and sellers were bundled back into South Street.

A large number of bosses and carvings of the original structure, discovered during the recent excavations, have been skilfully incorporated by Mr. Pearson in his restoration. Above the cloisters is a library containing 8,000 volumes, many of them bequeathed by the late Chancellor Harrington.

The Palace is a building so closely associated with the cathedral as to demand a brief notice. In it is the chapel of St. Mary, which seems to have been frequently used in preference to the cathedral for the celebration of episcopal functions. Ordination services were often held within its walls. It was originally built that services might be said there for the repose of the souls of dead bishops of Exeter. A document is quoted by Oliver, in which the parish of Alwyngham is called upon to pay the officiating chaplain a yearly sum of four marks and that of Harberton two. This chapel, now restored, is used for domestic purposes. But at one time it was clearly regarded as a portion of the cathedral, for the Dean and Chapter, on the festival of St. Faith, presented to it a pair of wax candles. Brantyngham, in 1381, mentions the "fructus et proventus cantariae infra Palatium nostrum Exonie, pro animabus predecessorum nostrorum ipsius fundatorum." The old entrance was under the great archway, and battlements, by gracious permission of royalty, surrounded the whole. In the great hall feasts were held for 100 poor people; but the palace now is shorn of a good deal of its grandeur. The Ecclesiastical Commissioners in 1845 decided to rebuild and repair what remained.

On the west side of the palace, and attached to it, a prison stood for scandalous and felonious priests. This was not, however, an unique appendage, for Archbishop Boniface commanded that there should be at least one such prison in every diocese : "Quilibet episcopus habeat in suo episcopatu unum vel duos carceres ad clericos flagitiosos, vel convictos juxta censuram canonicam detinendos." But in spite of a law for the perpetual imprisonment of the most deeply offending clerks, they sometimes managed to escape. After six felons, in 1389, had murdered the jailer and run away, the king gave Bishop Brantyngham his pardon, apparently because they were men of such "desperate villainy."

THE BISHOP'S PALACE.

THE FABRIC OF THE CATHEDRAL.

THE INTERIOR.

FINE as is the exterior, the interior of the building is quite as beautiful. Restoration of an unusually careful and discreet style has done much to revive the deteriorated splendours of the place. Sixty years ago the nave was filled with hideous and cumbersome pews, and such work as had been done towards keeping the place in repair was in the worst possible taste. But a change has been wrought of the happiest kind in recent years, so that no cathedral in the country can boast a more admirable interior.

It has been the custom to deplore the lack of elevation, and its lowness has compelled comparisons with the cathedrals of France. But this objection is, surely, rather trivial. For though the long vaulted roof, uninterrupted the whole length of the building, might tend to take away from the appearance of height, the work on the roof itself, the delicate ornaments on capitals and windows, do much to atone for this effect. To the ordinary visitor, it may safely be asserted, lack of height will only be obvious when pointed out to him.

The Nave.—Little of the Norman masonry is now to be seen, yet it is clear that when Marshall completed Warelwast's design he found the nave finished. To quote Canon Freeman, whose book, too technical for the general public, is of incalculable value to the student: "On the interior face of both north and south walls of the nave aisles, disturbances of masonry occurring at regular intervals indicate the position of a series of Norman pilasters, the base of one of them having recently been found *in situ* beneath the stone seat. Outside, and corresponding to the position of each several pilaster, may be observed either flat buttresses of Norman form and masonry, or else traces of their removal. These remains, linking together the obviously Norman towers and the massive west wall, point to the conclusion that the Norman cathedral, as Marshall found it, included the entire nave."

When the changes began, the Fabric Rolls, if they "do not entirely desert us," give us but meagre help, so that the exact date and cost of each detail is only to be guessed at. Stapledon probably intended, as early as 1325, to begin the work of recasting the nave. In that year he made purchases of "15 great poplar trees bought for scaffolds, and 100 alder trees." Further entries tell us of seven and eightpence worth of timber "bought by the Bishop at London," and "48 great trees from Langford." The work hitherto attempted by Stapledon did not demand an outlay of this kind; so, though Grandisson gets the honour of having finished the nave, something is due to Stapledon for having given the initiative. The large balances of the preceding nine years had left a great sum of money in the latter's hands, and a donation of Stapledon's further increased that balance by the substantial sum of £600. In January, 1333, is a record of William Canon's bill for marble he had been commissioned to furnish. He had agreed to supply the Purbeck pillars for the nave, receiving £10 16s. for eleven large columns, and 5s. a-piece for bases and capitals. This is one of the most interesting items we have of the building and cost of the cathedral, and occurs fortunately at a time when such information is unusually scanty. In addition to the above-mentioned Purbeck marble, stone from the quarries of Caen in Normandy, and other places nearer home, was procured in large quantities. In 1338 the bishop gave permission to the Dean and Chapter to obtain from his agents at Chudleigh "twelve suitable oaks from his wood there." About 1350 the building of the nave was completed. It was extensively restored in recent years under the guidance of Sir Gilbert Scott. The Purbeck columns had fallen into a most dilapidated state, and were carefully repaired, the material used being obtained from those spots which had supplied the original builders.

The view of the nave as one enters the west door is most impressive. Its full height of seventy feet is not dwarfed by the unhindered stretch of roof. The groined or wood roof itself is of marvellous beauty and springs from slender vaulting shafts, of which the bosses are exquisitely carved with a strange mixture of religious and legendary figures, foliage and animals. The artists seem to have ransacked the whole universe for sub-

jects, and to have interpreted their ideas with great cunning. The corbels that support the vaulting shafts are equally elaborately carved.

They consist of figures and foliage, and the variety of subjects chosen is no less surprising than the skill the artists have shown in the realization of their ideas. Whether they are peculiar to Exeter or not, it may be safely said that one could not easily find their equals either in design or execution. The subjects treated are too numerous for detailed treatment in this place, but the carving of vines and acorns and oakleaves will be readily admired.

The Photochrom Co. Photo.
THE MINSTRELS' GALLERY.

The nave is supported by thirty clustered pillars of Purbeck marble, showing various tints of blue and gray. The bases of the pillars are of three courses of moulding, and the capitals, though very simple, are admirably carved. On corbels of beautifully wrought foliage rise fourteen wide arches, seven on each side, graceful in form and rich with mouldings corresponding with the arrangement of the pillars that support them. The triforium, in groups of four arches under each bay, is unusually low, and rests on small clustered columns, broken in one place only on the north side to make way for the Minstrels' Gallery.

The Minstrels' Gallery.—This is the most beautiful gallery of its kind to be found in England, its twelve decorated niches containing figures of musicians. The musical instruments represented include the cittern, bagpipe, hautboy, crowth, harp, trumpet, organ, guitar, tambour, and cymbals, with two others which are uncertain. The tinted figures of the angels, standing out against an orange-coloured background, each in a separate niche topped by an elaborately carved canopy, playing upon the various instruments, are admirably carved and most graceful in form and arrangement. The two niches on either side of the gallery contained figures of St. Mary and St. Peter; the niches are supported by corbelled heads of Edward III. and Queen Philippa. Edward III. created the Black Prince Duke of Cornwall in 1337, and made the city of Exeter part of the duchy. "The city," according to Izacke, "being held of the said duke, as parcel of the dutchy, by the fee farm rent of twenty pounds per ann." To this connection has been traced the erection of the gallery, for such duchies "were territorial realities," and the prince would be received by minstrels chaunting in the gallery whenever he paid a visit to his feudal dependency. It is asserted that it was first used after the battle of Poictiers, when the Black Prince brought with him to England, visiting Exeter *en route* for London, the captured French king. But Professor Freeman thinks the Duke did not pay a visit to Exeter at that time, and that local tradition refers really to a later date when "he came home as a sick man" not long before his death.

The lofty character of the clerestory above the gallery, and set somewhat further back, is remarkable. The triforium, as we have already noticed, is unique in exactly the opposite way, being unusually low.

Windows of Nave.—The tracery of the windows is of the pure Decorated style, said to be unrivalled by those of any cathedral in the kingdom. Though they are arranged in pairs, there is no stern uniformity of design in each pair. In their main attributes the opposite windows tally, but in minuter details they differ.

Unfortunately, that which first demands our attention, the great west window, is a strange blending of excellence and ugliness, owing to the wretched glass inserted at the deadest period of church art, the middle of the last century. It is said that the ruby glass was the last, before the revival, manufactured in this country. One can only regret that the power of con-

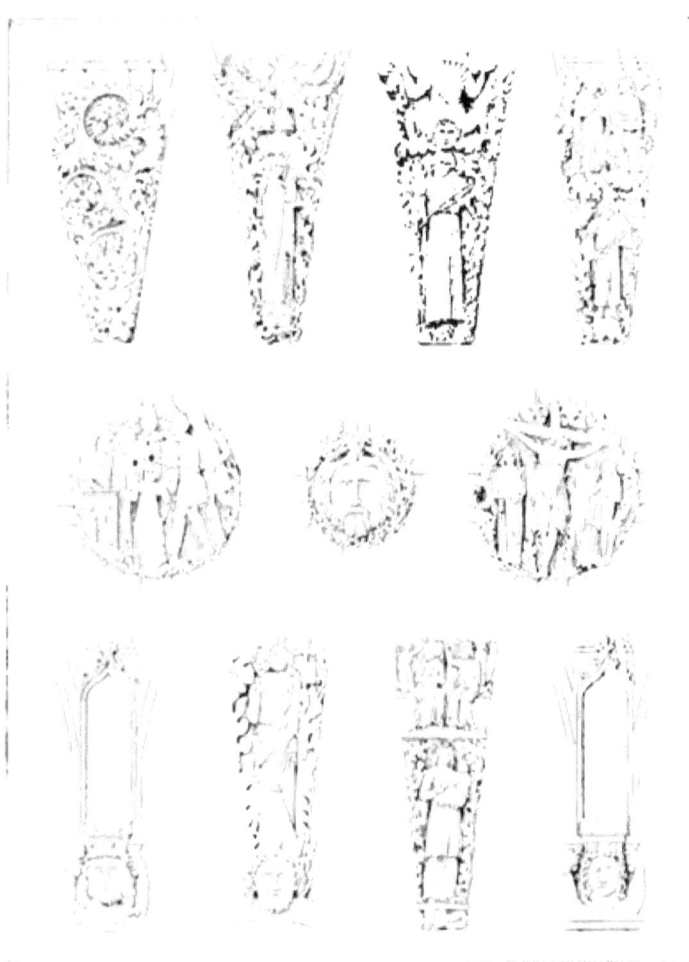

BRACKETS AND BOSSES IN EXETER CATHEDRAL (FROM BRITTON'S "EXETER," 1826).

triving so much ugliness had not died before the exquisite tracery was ruined by its vulgarity and crudeness.

It is said that a Mr. Peckett of York, who is responsible for the outrage, charged nearly a thousand guineas, and no one, it seems, was moved to complain of the expense. Certainly the number of subjects delineated does credit to Mr. Peckett, for in addition to figures of the evangelists, the armorial bearings of the royal family, the shamrock, the fleur-de-lis, the Agnus Dei, and the shields of the nobility, are not forgotten. But the horrid jumble of colours and subjects should not prevent the visitor admiring the exquisite tracery, so admirably in keeping with the rest of the architecture of the building, and of the fairest decorated character.

Monuments in Nave.—The first monument to notice is that under the west window, erected in honour of the 32nd (D. C. L. I.) regiment. This regiment greatly distinguished itself at Cawnpore and Lucknow, and the monument commemorates those who fell in defence of these cities.

In the North Aisle.—Above a mural tablet to Lieutenant G. A. Allen is a window of stained glass erected to the memory of the 11th Earl of Devon. The colour scheme is particularly good, and the design, representing Jacob's dream, is not unsuccessful.

Further on is a large brass, of no particular merit, to the memory of the men of the 2nd battalion of the North Devon regiment, who fell in the Afghan War of 1880-81. It is surmounted by two regimental flags, on one of which is "Salamanca."

The largest monument in the aisle, one, too, which attracts attention as much by reason of its singularly ugly design as by its size, is that to the memory of those officers and men of the 9th Lancers who fell in India. The two horses are well enough designed, but are too large for the purpose, and the desert of marble that separates them is unredeemed by a single graceful attribute. A plain and not very admirable tablet to the memory of Samuel Sebastian Wesley, the famous musician, is the only other monument it is necessary to notice.

Crossing the nave by the choir screen, the first monument that attracts attention at the east end of the south aisle is that of John Macdonald, F.G.S., a descendant of the famous Flora Macdonald. The figures in demi-relief are

THE NAVE, LOOKING EAST.

worth looking at, though the general effect is heavy and uninteresting.

In the first eastern bay is the Courtenay window, in memory of the famous Devonshire family. The traceries are enriched with the arms of the family and the heraldic devices of those with whom the family had allied itself. The fact that Bishop Courtenay received the Great Peter bell from Llandaff, giving for it five bells of Exeter, is commemorated in the bell design on the glass. The tomb of Hugh Courtenay is now in the south transept, but originally stood in a chantry near this spot. In or before 1630, however, the chantry was destroyed.

The brass to Sir Peter Courtenay, though considerably spoiled, is still beautiful. This Sir Peter was standard-bearer to Edward III., and won renown under the Black Prince in France and Spain, and followed "that manly exercise of Justs and Tournaments; now justled out of fashion by your carpet knights, who regard no Arms, but those which are for embraces." He was made a Knight of the Garter for his noble exploits by Richard II. (1390). The canopy and octofoils are still visible, and deserve most careful attention. The legend on the brass ran:

> "Devonie natus comes Petrusque vocatus
> Regis cognatus, Camerarius intitulatus,
> Calesia gratus, capitaneus ense probatus;
> Vita privatus fuit hinc super astra relatus.
> Et quia sublatus de mundo transit amatus
> Coelo firmatus maneat sine fine beatus."

The following lines are an ingenious translation, though not very good poetry,

> "The Earl of Devonshire's son, Peter by name,
> Kin to the King, Lord Chamberlain of Fame,
> Captain of Calais, for Arms were approved;
> Who dying was above the stars removed,
> And well beloved, went from the world away
> To lead a blessed Life in Heaven for aye."

It was of the bishop of this family that Fuller wrote that he was the son of Sir Philip Courtenay, and "was first preferred Archdeacon then Bishop of Exeter, expending very much money in finishing the North Tower, giving a great (called Peter) Bell thereunto." Fuller adds, "it is much one of so illustrious Birth should have so obscure a Burial, Bishop Godwin confessing that he knew not whereabouts in his Church he lieth interred."

The large brass tablet, though, like too many of the memorials in the nave, unnecessarily large and far from meritorious in design, is not without interest. It is to the memory of Major-General Elphinstone, V.C., whose sad death in 1890 is well remembered.

Above a tablet of brass to Hugh, 2nd Earl of Devon, and his wife, is a window erected by Sir Edwin Watkin to the memory of Thomas Latimer. The small window to the left, erected by Dean Cowie in memory of his wife, should be noticed.

The Transepts.—We have already seen that the two great towers of the cathedral were in their nature transeptal from the beginning. But they were quite separated from the body of the church, the arches so connecting them being filled in with strongly built masonry, forming a complete wall. But Quivil, wishing to enlarge the interior of the building, took down these walls, and he set about altering the arches and converting them into the same Decorated style to match this work in the rest of the building. He also altered and transformed the Norman chapels that projected on the east side of each transept. In the north transept one window and two narrow doorways still betray their Norman origin. The open galleries in each transept are connected by a passage with the clerestory. This, too, is Quivil's work, and his windows in the two chapels of St. John and St. Paul, easily distinguishable by their wheel-shape, are interesting.

Here is Chantry's fine statue of the Devonshire artist Northcote, and a tablet to the memory of the men and officers of the 20th (Devon) regiment who fell in the Crimea. Visitors will notice with interest a fairly successful mural painting representing the resurrection, the soldiers in armour being drawn with considerable spirit.

The Clock. The most interesting monument of antiquity, in the north transept, is a thirteenth century clock. The Fabric Rolls of 1376 mention an expenditure of £10, "circa cameram in boreali turre pro horologio quod vocatur 'Clokke.'" Dr. Oliver suggests that in 1424 another clock was substituted, for painting which John Budde was paid

THE TRANSEPT, NORTH, SHOWING THE CLOCK.

the "large sum" of £3 14s. 4d. But it is quite probable that the older clock had only been restored, and there is reason to believe that the clock we now see is the one originally mentioned in the Fabric Rolls of 1376.

Britton thus describes it:

"On the face or dial, which is about 7 feet in diameter, are two circles: one marked from 1 to 30 for the moon's age: the other figured from 1 to 12 twice over for the hours. In the centre is fixed a semi-globe representing the earth, round which a smaller ball, the moon, painted half white and half black, revolves monthly, and by turning on its axis shows the varying phases of the luminary which it represents. Between the two circles is a third ball representing the sun, with a fleur-de-lis, which points to the hours as it daily revolves round the earth."

This clock represents that ancient and discredited theory of astronomy which regarded the earth as the centre of the universe. In 1760 an upper disc was added to mark the minutes.

The **South Transept** contains the most interesting collection of monuments in the cathedral. The monuments themselves have merit, and the people they commemorate were of "importance in their day." Though there is nothing here so beautiful as the tomb of Bronscombe, there is not one unworthy of attention, and not one person so honoured but has distinct claims on our regard. It will be confessed readily enough, that the system of erecting large unsightly tablets to people of but second-rate quality has done a great deal to destroy the effect of the interior not only of Exeter, but of many other churches. Westminster Abbey is quite spoiled by the indiscriminate manner in which memorial tablets and statues have been received within its walls. Were these always of some artistic value in themselves the system would still be a bad one. And, unfortunately, as a rule, the efforts of the sculptor are more than only unsatisfactory. Exeter has suffered less severely than many places, and the judicious rearrangement of many of the figures has done not a little to improve matters. The subject, of course, is a very delicate one, and it would be unadvisable now to remove memorials of long standing, even were it possible. But fortunately it is quite easy to prevent further disfigurements in the future; and the care and taste shown during the recent restoration, and the beauty of much of the later memorial work, encourage the belief that those in authority will order matters with discretion and good taste.

The first monument that claims attention is the tomb—so tradition has it—of Leofric on the east wall. There was a tradition that the first bishop of Exeter was buried here, owing to an inscription in the southern tower of the sixteenth century. But the legend is probably of as late origin as the inscription, though it is said Hoker only replaced an earlier monument. Hoker thus tells the story: "This Leofricus died an. 1073, and was buried in the cemetery or churchyard of his own church, under a simple or broken marble stone; which place, by the since enlarging of his church is now within the South Tower of the same, where of late, anno 1568, a new monument was erected to the memory of so good, worthy & noble a personage, by the industry of the writer hereof but at the charges of the Dean & Chapter."

In the corner at the south-east is the tomb of Bishop John the Chaunter, who died in 1191. He was for thirty years precentor of the cathedral, and was consecrated bishop by Baldwin, Archbishop of Canterbury, "preacher and pilgrim of the Crusade," and a native of Exeter. Bishop John assisted at the coronation of Richard I. He held the see for six years.

Sir Peter Carew, whose mural tablet is a conspicuous feature, was buried at Waterford in Ireland. He is one of the most distinguished members of an ancient western family. On the Whitsunday of 1549, the village of Samford Courtenay rose in revolt against the new prayer-book that Edward VI. had ordered to be used in the churches, and the whole diocese speedily followed the lead. The people swore that "they would keep the old and ancient religion as their forefathers before them had done." Sir Gawain Carew, Sir Peter Carew, and Sir Thomas Dennis, the sheriff, were busy in stemming the tide of rebellion. Efforts at compromise were useless. The people bitterly demanded the old religion, and called the new form of worship "a Christian game," while the Cornishmen declared that they, since "certain of us understand no English, utterly refuse the new English." Early in July a siege of five weeks' duration began. The wealth of the civic dignitaries stimulated the besiegers, who summoned the city to surrender three times, vowing that "they would enter by force and take the spoil of it," were their demands refused. There was dis-

INTERIOR OF TALBOT IN THE LAST CENTURY (FROM A PRINT IN THE BRITISH MUSEUM).

content and plotting within the walls, and food gave out. Many were eager to let in the rebels, and Hoker records that "but two days before the delivery of the city," the malcontents paraded the streets, crying out: " Come out these heretics and twopenny bookmen! Where be they! By God's wounds and blood we will not be pinned in to serve their turn: we will go out and have in our neighbours; they be honest good and godly men." But the principal citizens, though nurtured in the old faith, held out grimly for the king. The siege was raised by John, Lord Russell, whom Sir Peter had hastily summoned from Hinton St. George, in Somersetshire. Food was supplied to the city "by the special industry and travels of a thousand Welshmen under Sir William Herbert." Sir Peter, on his arrival in London, was threatened with hanging by the Lord Protector "as having caused the commotion by burning the barns at Crediton. He pleaded the king's letter under his hand and privy signet." But he escaped with difficulty, though he obtained from Lord Russell the lands of Winislacre as a reward. Later on he opposed Queen Mary's marriage with the King of Naples, and as Fuller puts it: "This active gentleman had much adoe to expedite himself, and save his life, being imprisoned for his compliance with Sir Thomas Wyate." He lived an active, reckless life to the last, closing his career by some "signal service" in Ireland. He was a brother of the Earl of Totnes. The handsome Elizabethan monument is to Sir John Gilbert, brother of the more famous Humphrey, and his wife, Elizabeth Chudleigh. He was one of the merchant adventurers and a half-brother of Raleigh. His relations with Exeter were very friendly, the merchants being keenly interested in their discoveries, for they hoped in far away Asia to get a new market for their cloth.

The monument to Hugh Courtenay, 2nd Earl of Devon, and his wife Margaret, has been removed here from the nave. The restoration of it is very partially successful, and it is often asserted that a great deal of its loveliness has disappeared under unskilful hands.

Heroes of later days are not forgotten in this gallant company, and a tablet on the east wall commemorates the men of the 32nd (Cornwall Light Infantry) who fell in the Indian Mutiny. The colours of the regiment show the names of Waterloo and Lucknow.

The Ambulatory.—Between the high altar and the Lady Chapel is the ambulatory. It is unique in that the shafts differ from those in other parts of the building, and the north and south windows, of the time of Bishop Bruere (thirteenth century) are lancet shape. The architecture throughout the retrochoir is Early Decorated.

Two old oak bible-boxes are attached, one to each pillar: though ugly and clumsy they are distinctly interesting.

The windows are modern and excellent. Messrs. Clayton and Bell have seldom done anything better. The colours are quite admirable and well blended. Two monuments of Jacobean work are well worthy of attention. Concerning Jacob Railard there is nothing to be learnt.

John Bidgood was "one of the most accomplished and beneficial physicians of his age," and was born in 1623. At the beginning of his college career he appears to have been incorrigibly lazy, and answered his tutor, who bade him imitate the example of a certain laborious student, wittily enough, "Let him study if he will; yet for all that you may buy all his works twenty years hence for a groat." He was deprived of his fellowship at Exeter College in 1648 "for drinking of healths to the confusion of Reformers." Like many another good man he had to suffer for his loyalty. He obtained his doctor's degree at Padua and won a great reputation as a skilful and humane practitioner. With the Restoration he obtained his Oxford degree but continued to practise in his native city. He died in his sixty-eighth year.

Both tablets are extremely beautiful. Luckily their position prevents them from jarring in any way with the earlier style of the building; and as examples of their own age, it would be difficult to surpass them.

St. Radegunde's Chapel.—On the south side of the main entrance and within the western screen is the chapel of St. Radegunde, one of the most interesting in the cathedral. As early as 1220 a deed belonging to the Chapter makes mention of this chapel "within St. Peter's cemetery," and is dated in the mayoralty of one Turbest and attested by the then bishop, Simon de Apulia. Grandisson, in accordance with the custom of his day, while completing the work of transforming the cathedral, looked out for a suitable place of burial for himself. He chose this chapel, and in 1350 the Fabric

BAYS OF NAVE, WITH THE MINSTRELS' GALLERY (FROM BRITTON'S "EXETER, 1826").

Rolls contain a reference to the glazing of the windows and the better securing of them with nine bars of iron. In accordance with a clause in his will, "Corpus vero meum volo quod sepeliatur extra ostium occidentale Ecclesiae Exon. ita celeriter sicut fieri poterit," his remains were placed under the low arch in the east of the chapel. Here they lay for many years, but in the later years of Elizabeth, apparently without creating any public indignation, his tomb was rifled and his ashes scattered to the "four winds." There seems to be no good reason why religious fanaticism should have caused the tomb of so great and good a man to be despoiled. Two interesting details are the carved figure of Christ on the roof and the holes in the stones from which the lamps were formerly hung.

St. Edmund's Chapel.—On the left of the nave, that is, the north side, and in the first bay, is the chapel of St. Edmund. It belongs to a period earlier than the nave—showing, indeed, traces of Marshall's work. Bishop Grandisson connected them. It presents few features of interest. In the "Inventory" of 1506 the chapel is spoken of as "Capella Sancti Edmundi supra ossilegium in Cemeterio," therefore Dr. Oliver suggests there may be a crypt here.

Sylke Chantry.—In the north transept. Sylke was a person of considerable importance in his day, and one who deserved and obtained no little honour from his contemporaries. He administered the affairs of the diocese as vicar-general during the absence of Bishop Courtenay, and also during that of Bishop Fox. In 1499 he was made precentor, and held that office till his death. The priests, grateful for the efforts he had made to further their comfort, decided to keep his obit. The abbot and convent of St. Mary of Cleeve, in Somersetshire, willing to show their sense of obligation to him and Canon Moore, gave yearly to the Dean and Chapter the sum of £6 13s. 4d. to be spent in celebrating their anniversary. Sylke's tomb represents a very ghostly figure with the epitaph, "Sum quod eris, fueram quod es, pro me, precor, ora." The chantry is in the style of the later Gothic, and is one of those "final touches" to the cathedral, Canon Freeman esteems so happily imparted to it.

St. Paul's Chapel.—On the east side of the north transept. Attributed to the time of Marshall or his immediate predecessors. On the tiles are the arms of Henry III.'s brother, Richard of Cornwall, who was created King of the Romans. It is used as a vestry for the lay choral vicars.

Chantry of the Holy Ghost. This is in the south tower, one of the most ancient portions of the cathedral. Freeman says the vaulting is "either Norman or Saxon." It is now unused. It was probably the place to which the Dean and Chapter retired when they had to deliberate on ecclesiastical matters.

This chapel contains the font (pseudo-classic in design, and of no especial beauty) used at the baptism of Henrietta, Duchess of Orleans, daughter of Charles I., who was born in the city of Exeter.

The Chapel of St. John the Baptist, on the east of the south transept, is similar in nearly all respects to the chapel of St. Paul in the north transept. Some of the glass in the windows was placed there at the recent restoration of 1870. The screen dividing it from the transept is Oldham's work. The chapel is now used as a vestry for the priest vicars.

St. James' Chapel.—In the aisle on the south of the choir. In the north aisle immediately opposite is the companion chapel of St. Andrew. It will be noticed how frequently one part balances another throughout the building. This chapel is partly Marshall's work. When the apsidal chapels were pulled down at the time the apse was destroyed, Marshall built the present chapels of St. James and St. Andrew. Bronscombe altered them considerably, and the first item in the Fabric Rolls is, "for 3 windows for St. James Chapel 8s. 9d. :

ST. JAMES' CHAPEL (DRAWN BY H. P. CLIFFORD).

THE NAVE, FROM THE SOUTH TRANSEPT (FROM BRITTON'S
"EXETER, 1826").

for glass 16s." This is the last year of Bronscombe's episcopate, and proves he had, at any rate, almost finished the renovation of this chapel. The most noticeable features are the upper chamber, and the magnificent but half-destroyed decorated monument popularly known as Leofric's tomb. The chapel contained two altars, one dedicated to St. James and the other probably to St. Thomas.

Bishop Oldham's Chantry. This chapel, dedicated to our Saviour, has been greatly admired. It was richly restored by Bishop Oldham, who also restored the Speke—or St. George—Chantry immediately opposite. It is to this bishop we owe the "delicate and elegant screening which imparts distance and veiling to all nine chapels and to Prior Sylke's chantry in the north transept." The walls and vaulting are richly decorated, and the panelling and rebus at the north-east corner contain a stately pun on the bishop's name, being decorated with owls. In accordance with his object in restoring the chapel, his body was buried there and his effigy lies in a niche of the south wall. Oldham was a part founder of Corpus Christi College, Oxford, by whose orders the chapel was unfortunately restored some years ago. He settled the arms of the see—gules, a sword erect in pale argent, pommelled and hilted or, surmounted with two keys in saltire of the last. He was a native of Manchester, founded the grammar school there, and held the post of warden. He was a man of very methodical habits, according to Hoker. He dined regularly at eleven, and supped at five. "To ensure precision he had a house clock to strike the hours and a servant to look after it. Should his lordship be prevented by important business from coming to table at the appointed time, the servant would delay the clocks striking the hour until he knew that his master was ready. Sometimes, if asked what was the hour, he would humorously answer, 'As your lordship pleaseth,' at which the bishop would smile and go away."

St. Gabriel's Chapel.—This chapel was transformed by Bishop Bronscombe (1257-1280). The vaulting has been re-coloured in conformity with the ancient tints and patterns. The chapel contained several monuments, but these have been removed to other parts of the cathedral. Bronscombe transformed the chapel that it might be used for his burial place. St. Gabriel was his patron saint, and he caused the day of the archangel to be celebrated with honours similar to Easter Day and Christmas Day. There is some old glass in the windows.

SCREEN OF ST. GABRIEL'S CHAPEL.

Note the kneeling figure of the bishop with the scroll, "O Sancte Gabriel Archangele, intercede pro gratia." The skilful restoration of the south window with pieces of old glass is one of the most happy results of later work in the cathedral.

The Lady Chapel.—It has been suggested that this chapel occupies the site of the choir in the old cathedral of Leofric. The earliest mention of it is in a deed of Bishop Brueres in 1237. It was entirely remodelled by Quivil. But the "two pointed arches with solid piers—totally different from any others in the Cathedral—dividing Lady Chapel from the side chapels," though their moulding has been altered very considerably in order to tally with a later style, show evidence of much earlier date. The shafts are of Purbeck marble, and the windows, arranged as in the nave, contain the last importation of glass from abroad, save that in the transeptal windows, used in the cathedral. The bosses in the eastern bay, with the evangelists' emblems and head of Christ, should be noticed. The elaborate fourteenth century reredos is the work of Grandisson. The central niche contained a figure of the Virgin, before which a lamp was suspended. The sedilia and double piscina on the south side are interesting.

The Lady Chapel contains several monumental tombs of interest. Beneath the arches conducting to the side chantries are the effigies of Bishops Bronscombe and Stafford. There is a similarity between the two monuments, due to the fact that the canopies are of the same date and decorated in the same manner.

Bronscombe's Tomb.—That on the south side is Bishop Bronscombe's, and was probably in the Gabriel Chapel originally. The lion upon which the bishop is treading is a clever bit of sculpture, and though the angels at the feet are more curious than beautiful, they have certain merit, and are more successful than the canopy which is of the same date. The colouring on the effigy must have been uncommonly splendid, and even the remnants of the patterns have not faded out of all beauty.

Stafford's Tomb, on the north side, has had to contend with severer enemies than old age, but shockingly as the effigy has suffered, it still preserves something of its original beauty and stateliness. The attitude is simple: the gloved hands of the bishop are joined over his breast in an attitude of prayer. The face is thin and ascetic, its saintly austerity being rendered more noticeable owing to the rich mitre that crowns the head. The folds of the robe are managed with a consummate simplicity and skill. In Leland's "Itinerary" the bishop's epitaph is preserved:

"Hic jacet Edmundus de Stafforde intumulatus,
Quondam profundus legum doctor reputatus,
Verbis facundus, Comitum de stirpe creatus,
Felix et mundus Pater hujus Pontificatus."

Tomb of Sir John and Lady Doddridge.—Sir John Doddridge came of an old Devonshire family, for in 1285 one

BISHOP BRONSCOMBE'S MONUMENT (FROM BRITTON'S "EXETER," 1826).

Walter Doddridge and his wife surrendered to the Dean and Chapter of Exeter a right of entrance into the close from their house in High Street. Fuller says of him that it were "hard to say, whether he was better artist, divine, Cure, or Common Lawyer, though he fixed on the last for his publick Profession." He was second justice of the King's Bench, and gained great renown as a judge of stern integrity. Sir John was three times married, the lady whose effigy is here represented being his third wife, Dorothy, daughter of Sir Amias Bampfylde. She

The Photochrom Co., Photo.

THE LADY CHAPEL.

died in 1615. Sir John, who became a judge of the King's Bench, lived till 1628. He won the nickname of the "sleepy judge," for he always closed his eyes in court, the better to keep his attention fixed on the case. The monument is very elaborate, the effigy of Lady Doddridge being a master medley of ruff, wig, head-gear, roses, and carnations. But it is not so much beautiful as ingenious.

Tomb of Barthomæus Iscanus (died 1184).—The effigy, in low relief, is crude but impressive. A Norman helmet covers the head. The bishop wears a beard. The figure is in armour, but its ecclesiastical character is preserved by the position of the right arm, the first and middle finger being raised to bless. The left hand holds the pastoral staff, the point of which impales a winged dragon, with a sphinx-like head, at his feet. In the angles of the archway at the tomb are the figures of two angels with censers.

Tomb of Simon de Apulia (died 1223).—This is next to that of Iscanus, and presents a remarkable contrast to the work of a hundred years earlier. The great advance made in the art of sculpture is noticeable in the more human character of the face, which is clean shaven, and the more skilful management of the hands. The artist, too, seems to have courted difficulties, for the bishop's robe and mitre are richly jewelled, and the foliage and animal at his feet, though conventional, are most elaborately designed.

Bishop Peter Quivil (1291).—This tombstone in the centre of the pavement was restored here in 1820 on the representation of Mr. John Jones of Franklyn; the cross and letters were re-cut under his directions. The epitaph is "Petra tegit Petrum, nihil officiat sibi tetrum," and Westcott in his "View of Devon" writes, "which verse was written in an ancient character, each letter distant from the other at least four inches; so that this short verse supplied the whole large circumference, and cost me some labour in finding out and reading it."

Certainly this is one of the most interesting memorials in the cathedral; indeed, it may be well considered the most interesting, for it is dedicated to the man by whose genius the whole great design was begotten. Its simplicity is noteworthy. But Quivil required no elaborate sepulture; the cathedral itself is his mighty monument, since it was he who founded

"A fane more noble than the vestal trod—
The Christian's temple, to the Christian's God."[1]

St. Mary Magdalen Chapel, first mentioned in the Fabric Rolls for 1284. It was probably Marshall's work originally, Bronscombe further improved it, and Quivil entirely remodelled it. With the exception of the Perpendicular screen shutting it off from the north aisle, it is of the same date as the Lady Chapel. The north window is Bronscombe's work, and the still finer east window, containing a good deal of the early fifteenth century glass, is Quivil's. The chapel originally contained an altar to St. John the Evangelist and a figure of the Magdalen, for in Bishop Lacey's register are the words, " extra vestibulum coram ymagine Sanctae Mariae Magdalenae." On the floor of the chapel is a brass to Canon Langton, dated 1413. He was a cousin of Bishop Stafford. He is represented kneeling, clothed in a most rich cope and alb, on which is designed the Stafford knot. His hands are met in prayer. The epitaph only gives the date of his death, and refers to his relationship with the above-named bishop.

In this chapel also is a magnificent monument to Sir Gawain Carew and his wife, and their nephew, Sir Peter. It is in two parts: on the upper lie the figures of Sir Gawain and his dame, on the lower that of the more famous nephew, with his legs crossed, a unique position for a figure on so late a tomb. Sir Peter and his uncle took an active part in quashing the rebellion that disturbed the western counties in the reign of Edward VI. The former died at Waterford, in Ireland, 1575. Sir Peter Carew sat on the King's Commission of 1552, which summoned the Dean and Chapter to the bishop's palace, "then and there to answer all demands and questions concerning the jewells plate and other ornaments of your cathedrall churche."

In 1857 the monument was admirably restored by the members of the Carew family, the whole being gilded and coloured.

Speke's Chantry.—To the north-west of the St. Mary Magdalen Chapel, facing St. Saviour's: also called St. George's Chapel. It is of late, and exceedingly rich, Perpendicular work. A door opening on to the close completely spoils the effect. Oliver notices that in 1657 the east window and altar

---

[1] Richard Clarke Sewell, 1825, Magdalen College.

ST. GEORGE'S CHAPEL OR PERE'S CHANTRY. DRAWN BY H. P. CLIFFORD.

were destroyed to make a passage "into the great church of St. Peter's-in-the-East, partitioned from West Peter's by a brick wall erected, plastered, and whitened on both sides by Walter Deeble, at the expense of £150." The effigy of Sir John Speke rests in the chapel; the carving behind the figure is very elaborate. He hailed from White Lackington in Somersetshire. To secure the observance of his, and his wife's obit, he endowed the chapel with the "lands, tenements, and hereditaments in Langford, Frehead, and Ashill, in Somersetshire." The north window is to the memory of Archdeacon Bartholomew, and was placed here in 1865.

St. Andrew's Chapel.—Opposite to, and corresponding with that of St. James'. It was Marshall's work originally, like its fellow chapel, being a substitute for one of the old apsidal chapels of the Norman choir. Stapledon completed the renovations so as to make it a parallel to Bronscombe's restored chapel of St. James. The detached shafts are clearly an imitation of the earlier bishop's work. The chapel contains an upper chamber wherein are stored some of the muniments of the cathedral. Among the archives are Leofric's book, "with everything wrought poetry wise," MSS. of Roger Bacon, and the "Fabric Rolls," also the "Exon Domesday Book." Lacey's "Liber Pontificalis" and Grandisson's "Order of Services" have been removed to the chapter house. The chapel originally contained altars to St. Andrew and St. Catherine. In 1305 is an order of Bitton's that chantry services should be held here for Andrew de Kilkenny, late dean, and others. Among the names we find that of Henry de Kilkenny, who was at the time of Bitton's order still living, and a canon of the cathedral.

The Choir Screen.—This is the work of Bishop Stapledon, and was probably completed about 1324. The Dean and Chapter anticipated the admiration which this screen would cause in after ages, and we read that they presented William Canon, the executor of the marble work, "£4, out of their courtesy." This screen, it is suggested, was not really a rood screen at all, but built as a high and convenient place from which to read the gospels and epistles. The information supplied by the Fabric Rolls concerning the cost of its erection has led some to imagine they refer to an open-air structure for preaching from, as it is continually referred to

THE CHOIR, LOOKING WEST.

as "la pulpyte." But it is certain that the screen is meant, and its origin is French, and was probably built by French workmen.

ORGAN SCREEN, LOOKING N.E. (FROM BRITTON'S "EXETER," 1826).

None of the paintings within the small arches placed above the beautifully carved spandrils have any merit at all. Yet it is believed that they date from the same period as the screen itself. It is difficult, however, to believe that they can be so old, or that such good and bad work could belong to the same period. James I. introduced into the foliage of the spandrils the rose and thistle; but this atrocious emendation was summarily removed in the year 1875. The side arches of the screen were at one period filled up with thick walls and two strong doors barred the arch of entrance, but this was altered by the restorers in 1875.

The Choir.—If the chief glory with regard to the exterior of the cathedral remains undoubtedly with the designer and builder of the great towers, the choir, the work of Bitton and Grandisson, is no less certainly the supreme glory of the interior. The Norman choir reached no farther than the third bay, counting from the choir screen. Traces recently discovered seem to prove that it had an apsidal termination. Bishop Marshall, in completing Warelwast's work, added four bays and destroyed the triple apse. It is also possible that, as the transition period to Early English was in its birth, some of the vaulting was pointed. Bitton converted the choir as left by Marshall into the Decorated style, inspired in the work by the success which had attended Quivil's efforts in the easternmost bay of the nave. The whole work—the transformation of the choir with its aisles—took about fifteen years to complete, the speed and skill with which it was accomplished being due to the fact that the task was not entirely in the hands of one body of labourers. It seems to have been divided into two portions, at which the builders worked simultaneously. Admirable as Quivil's work in the nave had been, that of Bitton in the choir is an improvement. Doubtless he had learnt something from the difficulties his predecessor encountered, and knew how to avoid them. At any rate, he pushed forward the work with great vigour and boldness. He formed his pillars of horizontal sections of Purbeck marble from nine to fifteen inches thick: five boutelles on each side presenting "the appearance of twenty-five shafts bound in one." In the pavement of the choir more than ten thousand tiles were used. For the vaulting of the choir, also his work, though the honour due to him has till lately been denied, he procured quantities of Portland stone. Sixty capitals ready carved were imported also from Portland: the entry in the Fabric Rolls runs: "For the purchase of 18 great blocks of stone at Portland for the keys or bosses, together with 60 bases and capitals, including carriage by sea £4 16 8." The colouring of the key-

stones was accomplished by Stapledon in the first year of his episcopate. Between 1870-75 the choir underwent very extensive repairs. For the most part they were successful, and if in particular instances objection may be taken, it would be hypercriticism to detract from their value. Wherever possible, the stone was taken from the quarries used by the first builders. The Purbeck marbles especially had severely suffered, and the mouldings and bases ruthlessly destroyed for the better accommodation of the wainscoting to the stalls; moreover, the differences in the nature of the stone were rendered null by a hideous yellow wash with which they had been lavishly besprinkled. During the restoration the corbels and roof-bosses were cleaned and carefully repaired. These, though of the same character as those in the nave, are both richer and more varied in design and more skilfully carved.

The Choir Stalls. The stalls are entirely modern, and the work of Sir Gilbert Scott. Originally the stalls no doubt were similar in style to the bishop's throne, one of the rarest of Stapledon's additions to the cathedral. They were probably surmounted with canopies, with an open arcade of stone behind them. The modern designer has so constructed his stalls as to bear out this idea, since as far as possible they are meant to replace the earlier ones. The misereres of Bishop Bruere have been placed beneath the seats. These misereres have not their equal in England. They are richly carved, representing foliage, beasts such as lions and elephants, men fighting and playing musical instruments, and legendary monsters. These last should be specially observed, the grotesque lending itself admirably to the somewhat stiff manner of the artist who carved them. It is believed that the introduction of an elephant is quite unique, and it is presumed that as Bishop Bruere had lived some years in the East, he wished to reproduce some of the marvels he had seen. It certainly adds greatly to their value and interest, and the restorer has been well advised in accepting the hint and taking his cue, as regards the modern work, from the thirteenth century bishop.

The Reredos.—This, too, is modern work, and most successfully has Earp carried out the designs of Sir Gilbert Scott. It is of alabaster, inlaid with agate, cornelian, and jasper. In the centre of the three compartments into which it is divided is the Ascension, the other two groups representing the Descent from the Cross and the Transfiguration. As the work has met with considerable opposition, it is well to remember Canon Freeman's words, he having the best of all rights to speak. "With its delicate canopies of alabaster, and sculptures wrought in bold relief, its inlay of choice marbles, its redundance of costly stones, and its attendant angel figures, it enshrines a multitude of ideas well harmonizing with its place and purpose." The ancient altar of Stapledon's has long since disappeared. This was mostly of silver, the mensa only being of marble. In the monument of Leofric, erected by Hoker, the historian, was found a large slab of marble marked with crosses. This probably was a portion of Stapledon's altar destroyed by an Order in Council, 1550.

The Throne.—For a great number of years this superb piece of work was attributed to Bishop Bothe. Dr. Oliver says: "Whether there be sufficient grounds for the tradition that the bishop was the donor of our episcopal throne we cannot pronounce; but it is evidently of the character of the time." Now this is obviously wrong. It is Stapledon's work, as the entries in the Fabric Rolls show: "for timber for the bishops seat £6. 12. 8½." The carving, too, appears to be of the same date as the choir, and would not be so wonderfully good were it an imitation.

At the date of the 1870 restorations the throne was in a very parlous state. It had been covered with brown paint, and the lower panels were not a little damaged. There are traces of colouring still, but no attempt has been made, and wisely, to restore them. Only the paintings at the base have been renovated, which commemorate the quartette of famous bishops, Warelwast, Quivil, Stapledon, and Grandisson. The height of the throne is 57 feet, and the carving is most elaborate. Originally the niches of the tabernacle work were filled with figures, but these have disappeared.

The Sedilia.—It is natural after an examination of the throne in wood to turn to Stapledon's still more splendid achievement in stone. The sedilia were most carefully restored under Sir Gilbert Scott. There are three arches, each 50 feet high, of open work, above which is a rich display of tabernacle work. The niches once contained statues, for the sockets are visible. The carving, extraordinarily skilful and intricate, consists of leaves and animals' heads. Like much of the carving

THE CHOIR BEFORE RESTORATION (FROM AN ENGRAVING AFTER CHARLES WILD).

in the cathedral that is attributed to this date, it was the work of De Montacute, a French artist. The seats are divided by metal shafts, the terminal divisions being supported by lions. It has been contended that these lions are of considerably earlier date than the rest of the work; but there is no evidence

THE "PATTERSON" PULPIT.

to go upon except a fancied resemblance to Early English work. But lions are not unpopular features of sacred and ecclesiastical decoration as a sign of Christian courage, and the mildest of the evangelists, St. Mark, is for ever commemorated by it, concerning which a well-known author has written: "How wonderful would he have thought it, that by the lion symbol

SEDILIA IN THE CHOIR.

in future ages he was to be represented among men! how woful, that the war-cry of his name should so often reanimate the rage of the soldier, on those very plains where he himself had failed in the courage of the Christian and so often dye with fruitless blood that very Cypriote sea, over whose

PULPIT IN THE CHOIR.

waves, in repentance and shame, he was following the Son of Consolation." Of course the question may never be settled, but there seems no reason why Stapledon should not have chosen lions as a fitting decoration, and carved them in a style more or less traditional. The small heads are sometimes considered coeval with the lions and earlier than the canopy. Three small heads are carved on the back of each seat, the centre one being that of Leofric, and on either side the heads of Edward the Confessor and his wife Eadgytha. It will be remembered that they were present, with their whole court, at the installation of Leofric as first bishop. The sedilia were for long known as "Bishop Leofric's stone," and there is an entry in the year 1418 recording that twenty pence was paid "for writing on the stone of my Lord Leofric." There was certainly no monument to the bishop, or at any rate none recognizable by any inscription, for Hoker erected and inscribed one at his own cost in the seventeenth century, utilizing part of the dismantled altar for the purpose. The sedilia must clearly be meant by this entry, therefore, more particularly as traces of scroll-work have been discovered at the back of it.

On the triforium arcading, just over the sedilia, the heads of Leofric, Edward, and Eadgytha are repeated.

The Choir Vaulting.—This is the work of Messrs. Clayton and Bell. The attempt to give back to the roofing by gilding the bosses and painting the ribs red and blue and gold, while the ground colour is a dull white, is not without merit. But perhaps it errs on the side of having retrained from tempting failure. It only approximately reproduces the effect which was originally obtained, but no doubt much of its tone has been restored. Unfortunately, the clerestory windows do not aid the general effect, but in some measure spoil it.

The East Window.—Henry de Blakeborn, a canon of the cathedral, enlarged "this Gable window in the Perpendicular style." Although it was damaged a good deal in Cromwell's time, much of the old glass remains. The shields on the upper part of the window are modern, but those at the bottom are those of the first bishops and benefactors. The three centre figures in the lowest row were added in Brantyngham's day.

TOMBS IN THE CHOIR AND CHOIR AISLES.

THE first tomb to notice on the north side of the choir is that of the murdered bishop, Stapledon. The canopy was judiciously restored at the beginning of the century. From beneath it one observes a great image of Christ, the pierced hands raised to bless. The wounded feet stand upon a sphere, possibly to represent His dominion over the world, and an insignificant earthly king, in scarlet robes, seems to take refuge in the shadow of the Saviour. Beneath the canopy lies the figure of the bishop, grasping the crozier in his left hand and a crook in his right. The keys upon his sleeve represent the arms of the see. Above the monument the arms of the bishop figure on the choir screen, and over the tombs of Lacey and Marshall the same plan has been observed. This screen was erected about the close of the Fourteenth century.

The next tomb, that of Marshall, is of peculiar interest, and it is unfortunate that a good view is not easily attainable. It has been pointed out by a specialist that the ornament on the cope is almost unique, reminding one of the foliage in Early English work. The medallions at the side are especially interesting. A plain slab commemorates the saintly Bishop Lacey, and it was here that the miracles we have elsewhere referred to were said to be accomplished.

The Choir Aisles are still richer in monuments that demand somewhat careful attention. For they not only possess genuine artistic and antiquarian merits, but are the records in stone of most notable people. The first that attracts one's curiosity in the North Choir Aisle is the effigy of a knight whose legs are crossed, and whose armour fixes the date of the sculpture to the first half of the fourteenth century. It is generally supposed to be the tomb of Sir Richard de Stapledon, an elder brother of the great bishop whose tragic death we have already described in the first chapter of this book. He was a lawyer and one of his Majesty's judges. Prince's quaint description of his tomb is worth quoting in full: "In a niche in the wall is a monument erected to his Memory, representing his Figure lively cut in stone sitting on horseback; where is cut out also in the same, a cripple taking hold of the foreleg of his horse: which seems to confirm the Tradition, That a certain Cripple, as Sir Richard was riding into the City of London with his Brother, lying at the gate, laid hold on one of his Horse's

TOMB OF BISHOP STAPLEDON.

Fore legs, and by crossing of it threw Horse and Rider to the Ground; by which means he was soon slain: and that from this occasion the place obtain'd the name of Cripple-gate, which it retains to this day." It is a pity so quaint a story belongs to the realm of legend, for there is no substantial proof forthcoming of its truth.

The skeleton, as Oliver calls it, placed within a niche, is often taken to be a memorial of Bishop Lacey. This, however, is a mistake, as Lacey's tomb is on the north side of the choir, and will be referred to later. The tradition had its origin possibly from the frequency of such memorials in our cathedrals: and

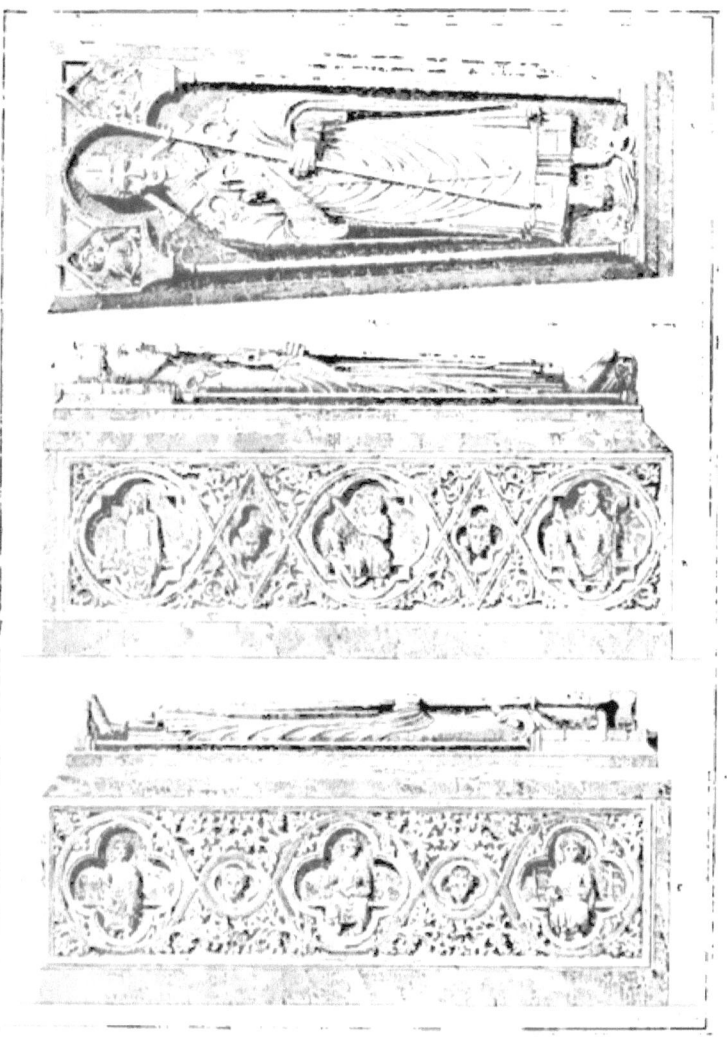

MONUMENT OF BISHOP MARSHALL (FROM BRITTON'S "EXETER," 1826).

Oliver reminds us that Fox desired to be commemorated in this manner in his chantry at Winchester. The monument to Anthony Harvey of Colomb John is of no great interest, being poorly designed. Its date is 1564. Harvey was steward of the abbeys of Hartland, Buckland, and Newenham at the time when the religious houses were suppressed. He is said to have amassed very considerable wealth; for, in addition to the profits derived from the spoliation of the above monasteries, he received from Henry VIII. considerable lands belonging to the abbey of Tewkesbury, which he sold, probably most advantageously, to a clothier of Crediton. Why, save on account of his wealth, he was buried in the cathedral, is not very apparent. Two tablets, to Robert Hall, a son of the bishop, and Canon Rogers, are of no particular interest.

The South Choir aisle possesses two effigies that excite a melancholy interest. They are those of two knights who have won renown in the crusades, for their legs are crossed: yet not a trace remains of their victories and their titles—the visitor must invent them for himself. They are striking sermons on the brevity of human glory, the weakness of human memory.

Incited by a worthy anxiety to save them from oblivion, they have been held by some to be memorials of Sir Humphrey de Bohun, but the suggestion is mere conjecture. Others again say they are Knights of the famous west country family of Chichester. Here the wish is, unfortunately, only father to the thought.

Concerning these tombs or effigies, there is a very interesting chapter in Cotton and Woollcombe's "Municipal and Cathedral Records," headed "Sir Henry Ralegh de Ralegh." It is there contended that the one furthest east was placed there by the 2nd Countess of Devon to Humphrey de Bohun, Earl of Hereford and Essex. The other is alleged to be the memorial of Ralegh de Ralegh. The argument may be outlined thus. The arms on the monument are those of the Chichester family. But the Chichester family, only after the monument was erected, adopted the Ralegh arms. On a day in 1301 the body of Henry de Ralegh was laid out in the church of the Black Friars, awaiting interment. The cathedral clergy claimed that the body should be laid out in the cathedral, and masses said over it there. The friars, following the wishes of the deceased knight, refused compliance. Thereupon the

Exeter Cathedral.

Dean and Chapter had the body forcibly seized and carried off to the cathedral. There the usual ceremonies were performed. But the insulted friars refused to take back the body and receive it for burial. So it had to be carried back to the cathedral and there entombed. The story, dating but a few years after the murder of Walter Lochlade, referred to in Chapter I., gives a curious account, and exact, of the rough manners of the age. And it is worth telling for that reason, even if it be inaccurate as regards the identification of the dead knight.

Neither the effigy of Bishop Cotton (1621) nor the angel resting on the sarcophagus of Bishop Weston—a typical Georgian monument—are of much intrinsic merit. Flaxman's statue to General Simcox, the hero of the Queen's Rangers in the American War, is the only other notable monumental achievement in the south choir aisle.

The Peter, or Great Bell, of Exeter is said to have been a gift of Bishop Courtenay's. This opinion is very much disputed, as the Fabric Rolls show that there were bells here in the time of Edward II. As early as 1351 is an entry of 6s. for mending the Peter Bell. Again in 1453, twenty-five years before Courtenay was created bishop, mention is made of the spending of twenty pence "in una bauderick pro Maxima Campana in Campanili Boreali." Oliver, however, acutely points out that this last entry is dated the very year that Courtenay was appointed Archdeacon of Exeter, and suggests that "on that occasion he may have offered such valuable presents." On the 5th November, 1611, the bell was crazed, but was recast in 1676. Its reputed weight is 12,500 lb. If this is correct, it is the second largest bell in England. Great Tom of Christ Church, Oxford, is more than 5,000 lb. heavier, but it easily exceeds its other rivals, Tom of Lincoln and the Great Bell of St. Paul's, which weigh respectively 9,894 lb. and 8,400 lb.

THE DIOCESE OF EXETER.

A CHRONOLOGICAL list of the bishops of the diocese, from the days of Leofric, when the seat of the bishopric was removed from Crediton, to our own day, when the diocese of Truro has been carved out from that of Exeter, is here given briefly, since the more notable holders of the see have been already mentioned in the first chapter.

Leofric (1046-1072). In 1050 the see was removed from Crediton and the new See of Exeter founded.

Osbern (1072-1103). No alterations were made to the building during this period. The bishop was admired for his "simplicity of English manners and habits," for although Norman by birth he had been educated in England.

William Warelwast (1107-1136), a nephew of William the Conqueror, began to demolish the Saxon Church. To him may be attributed the towers, choir, apse, and nave of the Norman building. The story of his blindness, and of his being sent on an embassy to Rome, rests on somewhat slender authority.

Robert Chichester (1138-1155) was promoted from the deanery of Salisbury at the Council of Northampton. He continued Warelwast's work.

Robert Warelwast (1155-1160) was a nephew of the former bishop of that name.

Bartholomæus Iscanus (1161-1184), a native of Exeter, was of humble birth. He is said to have been an enemy of Becket's and was called by Pope Alexander III. "the luminary of the English Church."

John the Chaunter (1186-1191) continued the buildings which had been suspended during the last episcopate.

Henry Marshall (1194-1206), brother to the Earl of Pembroke, Marshal of England, was promoted from York, of which cathedral he was dean. He completed the buildings as designed by the first Warelwast. To him we owe the Lady Chapel, the larger choir, the north porch, cloister doorway, and six chapels. He assisted at the coronation of King Richard at Winchester in 1194, and at that of John in 1199.

Simon de Apulia (1214-1223). But little is recorded of this bishop. He assisted at Henry III.'s coronation at Gloucester when the king was a lad of ten. To him also is attributed the fixing of the boundaries of the city parishes. His tomb is in the Lady Chapel.

William Bruere (1224-1244) served as Precentor of Exeter before he was made bishop. To him are due the chapter house and stalls in the old choir. For five years he was in the Holy Land, and Matthew Paris writes of his energy and untiring devotion in administering to the wants of his countrymen.

Richard Blondy (1245-1257). According to Hoker this bishop was the son of Hilary Blondy, Mayor of Exeter in 1227.

Walter Bronescombe (1257-1280), a native of Exeter, was only in deacon's orders when chosen bishop. He restored the chapels of St. Gabriel, St. Mary Magdalene and St. James. He also founded a college at Glasney and restored "the establishment of Crediton" to much of its former splendour.

Peter Quivil (1280-1291) was born in Exeter, and a *protégé* of Bronescombe's. His first preferment was as Archdeacon of St. David's, from whence he was promoted bishop of his native city. He it was who designed the Decorated cathedral and transformed transepts with chapels, eastern bay of the nave, and the Lady Chapel.

Thomas de Bytton (1292-1307) continued Quivil's work, transforming the choir and its aisles. He was a native of Gloucestershire and had been Dean of Wales. An indulgence of forty days was granted by the Pope, Boniface VIII., three archbishops and five bishops, to all who should pray for his prosperity. The rules he made for the government of the collegiate church at Crediton won general approval.

Walter de Stapledon (1308-1326) was Professor of Canon Law at Oxford and a chaplain to Pope Clement V. He was killed by a London mob. The transformed choir transepts are his work, and he erected the organ screen, bishop's throne, and sedilia. During his episcopate, also, the cloisters were begun.

James Berkley (1326-1327), Archdeacon of Huntingdon, and grandson of William de Ferrers, Earl of Derby, died a few weeks after his consecration.

John Grandisson (1327-1369) was born in Herefordshire, of good family. His long tenure of the see is one of the most memorable chapters in the history of Exeter Cathedral and city, and has been dealt with in an earlier chapter. He inherited the transforming zeal of his predecessors and set his seal on the six western bays of the nave, the great west windows, and the vaulting and the aisles. He completed the north cloister.

Thomas Brantyngham (1370-1394) was educated at the Court of Edward III., and was a canon of Exeter when chosen bishop. He was a constant adviser of the king, only being released from his privy council and parliamentary duties when his advanced age made them irksome to him. He was very busy in all the affairs of the diocese, but found time to complete the cloisters, east window, and west front.

Edmund Stafford (1395-1419) came of a greatly distinguished family. He was a canon of York when Pope Boniface IX. advanced him to the See of Exeter. For a time he served the king as Lord High Chancellor. He has been abused by Campbell in his "Lives of the Lord Chancellors of England": but there seems little doubt that he deserved the reputation he certainly got of being learned, grave, and wise, and "very well accounted generally of all men." To him are attributed the canopies over the tombs in the Lady Chapel.

John Ketterick or **Catterick** (1419) died at Florence a month after his appointment.

Edmund Lacey (1420-1455), composer of an office in honour of the Archangel Raphael, left a saintly reputation, and pilgrimages were, for long, made to his tomb. According to Canon Freeman he raised the chapter house and glazed the nave windows.

George Neville (1458-1465) was a son of the Earl of Salisbury. He was Chancellor of Oxford, and only twenty-four when made bishop. Though for several years Lord High Chancellor, and translated to York, he died in disgrace and comparative poverty.

John Bothe (1465-1478) was the son of a Cheshire

knight. He has often, but wrongly, been credited with being
the donor of the throne. With more certainty the roof of the
chapter house has been acknowledged as his work.

Peter Courtenay (1478-1486), son of Sir Philip Courtenay
of Powderham, had been Archdeacon of Exeter and Wiltshire,
and Dean of Windsor and Exeter before he was appointed
Bishop of Exeter. He assisted at the coronation of Richard III.,
but was none the less translated, for his services, by Henry to the
diocese of Winchester.

Richard Fox (1487-1491), the next bishop, was held in
great esteem by Henry VII., whom he represented for a time
as Ambassador at the Court of Scotland. He arranged the
preliminaries of the marriage of Henry's daughter Margaret with
James IV. He was translated to Bath and Wells, then to
Durham, and finally to Winchester. He is said to have refused
the dignity of Archbishop of Canterbury, which his godson,
Henry VIII., was anxious he should accept.

Oliver King (1492-1495) was Bishop of Exeter for a short
time, only being translated to Bath and Wells. He began building the Abbey Church at Bath, but did not live to see much of
it completed.

Richard Redman (1496-1501) was translated to Exeter
from St. Asaph. He resigned the see on becoming Bishop
of Ely.

John Arundell (1502-1503) was translated from the See of
Lichfield and Coventry. He was famous for his benevolence
and hospitality. He died after barely two years' tenancy of
the western bishopric.

Hugh Oldham (1504-1519) came of an ancient Lancashire family. A large and flourishing manufacturing town in
that county bears his name. He founded the grammar school
in Manchester, and on his elevation became famous throughout the west of England for his learning and piety.

John Vesey (Harman) (1519-1551). A lengthy account
is given of this bishop in the first chapter.

Miles Coverdale (1551-1553) was a famous reformer, and
revised Tyndale's translation of the Bible. He was not popular
in the diocese, and on Queen Mary's accession was deprived
of his see, to the great satisfaction of his flock.

James Turberville (1555-1559) was deprived of his see
on his refusal to acknowledge the ecclesiastical supremacy of

Elizabeth. He had been popular in the west of England, where the Reformation was at first heartily disliked.

William Alleyn (1560-1570). Oliver writes the surname Alley. The diocese was now so poor that he was compelled to reduce the number of canons from twenty-four to nine. Only by accepting the rectorship of Honiton was the bishop himself able to support the dignity of his office. He was the author of several religious books that had considerable popularity in their day.

William Bradbridge (1570-1578) is said to have speculated largely in agricultural land, and to have died a debtor for a large amount, including £1,400 owed to Queen Elizabeth. Beyond this little is recorded of him except that he lived at Newton Ferrers, which must have put his clergy to great inconvenience.

John Wolton (1579-1594). During Wolton's episcopate the revenues were restored to the chapter, the crown reserving to itself the sum of £145 yearly. The priest-vicars, also, received back from the queen the greater portion of their possessions.

Gervase Babbington (1595-1597) was translated from Llandaff. He remained at Exeter but a short time. He seems to have been a favourite with the queen, who took an early opportunity to promote him to the wealthy See of Worcester.

William Cotton (1598-1621).

Valentine Carey (1621-1626) had been Master of Christ's College, Cambridge, and Dean of St. Paul's.

Joseph Hall (1627-1641) was Dean of Worcester when promoted to the See of Exeter. He was a famous theological writer, and was translated to Norwich in 1641. There he suffered a great deal of unmerited persecution, which he bore bravely, though the ill treatment of his enemies killed him.

Ralph Brownrigg (1642-1659), Master of St. Catharine's, Cambridge, was bishop in troublous times. He had to retire to a friend's house in Berkshire. He was elected Preacher of the Temple, and was buried at the cost of the Inn.

John Gauden (1660-1662) was Master of the Temple. His title to fame is as the reputed author of the EIKΩN BAΣIΛIKH. Being the first bishop appointed after the Restoration, his arrival in Exeter was gladly welcomed by the loyal citizens. But he does not seem to have been a lovable man, and was over-eager for riches. He was translated to Worcester on his complaint of poverty reaching the king's ears.

Seth Ward (1662-1667) was already popular as dean when he succeeded Gauden as bishop. He cleared the cathedral of the small traders who desecrated the precincts, and gave to his church the finest organ then known in England. He was translated to Salisbury, and became Chancellor of the Order of the Garter. He obtained an enviable reputation for his good sense, piety, learning, and generosity.

Anthony Sparrow (1667-1676) was Master of King's College, Cambridge, when consecrated bishop. Cosmo III. visited Exeter during his tenancy of the see.

Thomas Lamplugh (1676-1688) seems to have been a clever politician. By expressing his loyalty to James II., when William had landed at Torbay, he was created Archbishop of York; thereupon he actively supported the Prince of Orange. "My Lord, you are a genuine old Cavalier," was the king's greeting. One hopes the memory of those words troubled the archbishop during his three years' experience of an ill-deserved dignity.

Jonathan Trelawney (1689-1707) came of a famous Cornish family. As Bishop of Bristol he was already famous, for he was one of the seven bishops whose trial and acquittal hastened the downfall of the last Stuart king. He was translated to Winchester. A popular refrain, wedded to verses by the celebrated parson Hawker, of Morwenstow, keeps his memory alive in the western counties.

Offspring Blackhall (1708-1716) was chiefly and honourably known as a promoter of charity schools.

Launcelot Blackburne (1717-1724). Of this bishop there is little to record. He was translated to the Archbishopric of York in 1724.

Stephen Weston (1724-1742). The episcopal registers were now kept for the first time in English. His long reign seems to have been quite uneventful, and probably was, therefore, entirely successful.

Nicholas Claggett (1742-1746) was translated from St. David's.

George Lavington (1747-1762).

Frederick Keppel (1762-1777), a son of the Earl of Albemarle, was a canon of Windsor when appointed Bishop of Exeter.

John Ross (1778-1792).

William Buller (1792-1796), of an old west country family, was promoted from the deanery of Canterbury.

Henry Reginald Courtenay (1797-1803), translated to this see from Bristol.

John Fisher (1803-1807) was tutor to the Duke of Kent, father of Queen Victoria. He was translated to Salisbury in 1807.

George Pelham (1807-1820) was translated from Bristol. After, according to Oliver, "for thirteen years expecting higher preferment," he was promoted to Lincoln.

William Carey (1820-1830), head master of Westminster School. When he had been ten years at Exeter he was translated to St. Asaph, a curious reversal of the usual proceeding. For although a Welsh bishopric often led to an English one, a change from Exeter to St. Asaph could hardly have been "promotion" in the ordinary sense.

Christopher Bethell (1830-1831). Exeter, for this bishop, was merely a stepping-stone between Gloucester and Bangor.

Henry Phillpotts (1831-1868) was the most famous bishop who has held the see in this century. He restored the palace, which had fallen into a ruined condition. He was energetic about the affairs of his diocese, a born ruler of men, and a scholar of eminence. The story of his episcopate is a well-known chapter to students of the ecclesiastical history of the first half of the queen's reign.

Frederick Temple (1869-1885), head master of Rugby, 1858-1869; Bishop of Exeter, 1869; translated to London, 1885, and to the Metropolitan See of Canterbury, 1896.

Edward Henry Bickersteth (1885-) was Dean of Gloucester when appointed bishop. He is the editor of the "Hymnal Companion," also the author of "Yesterday, To-Day, and For Ever," and many other popular works.

ROUGEMONT CASTLE AND THE GUILDHALL.

It is related that when Gytha fled towards the river and William the Conqueror marched through the eastern gate of the city, claiming it as his prize, he promised the citizens their lives, goods, and limbs. But, although he adhered strictly to his promise, and took care that his victorious soldiers should not pillage or insult the inhabitants, he was well aware of the supreme value of his conquest. The taking of Exeter was practically the taking of all western England. So he determined to make his position impregnable, and to this end set about the building of a castle on the Red Mount. The task was not a hard one: the Norman engineers had little need to display their peculiar ingenuity. Nature had done much, and to her work Briton, Roman, and Englishman had made additions. As Professor Freeman puts it: "The hillside was ready scarped, the ditch was ready dug." Baldwin de Molles was appointed superintendent and commander, and so well did he carry out his trust that within a year the castle was built and the men of Cornwall and Devon had attacked its walls in vain. Perhaps because William had been a merciful conqueror, not despoiling or ill-using the citizens, perhaps because the citizens were afraid, knowing the just man was strong and his hand heavy in anger, the besiegers found no help within the city walls. Henceforth Exeter was for the king.

A curious example of its loyalty was shown in the troubled days of King Stephen. Earl Baldwin, from all accounts a cruel and violent man, took arms against the king. Stephen demanded that the castle should be delivered up. For his answer the Earl laid in provisions, and at the head of his followers patrolled the streets of the city threatening vengeance on those who opposed his will. Stephen, speedily apprised by his faithful citizens of these riotous doings, sent two hundred

OLD HOUSES IN NORTH STREET.

knights to confront the rebel. Later he came himself, and the castle was closely besieged. After three months' heavy fighting the wells in the castle gave out. Deprived of water, Baldwin, who was brave enough, made shift with wine, using it both for cookery and extinguishing the fires. But at last the king was victorious and, not heeding the wise counsel of his brother Henry of Winchester, permitted the followers of Baldwin to "go forth with their goods and follow what lord they would."

In 1483, Richard III., fearing that the west favoured the claims of Henry, Earl of Richmond, hastened to Exeter. He was civilly greeted by John Attwill, the mayor. But his coming was not very welcome, nor did his conduct contribute to the gaiety of the inhabitants. In his train was Lord Scrope, whose business it was to try the rebels. None could be found, however, save the king's brother-in-law, St. Leger, and his esquire, John Rame. Richard none the less determined to strike terror into the hearts of all who wavered in their allegiance. So both men were beheaded at the Carfax. This done, the king busied himself in studying the surrounding country, and made careful note of the city and castle. The military strength of Rougemont pleased him, though the name did not. A west country accent, some say, gave it a sound like Ridgemount, too close an echo of his rival's title. The incident is referred to by Shakespeare in these well-known lines :

> "Richmond! when I last was at Exeter,
> The mayor in courtesy showed me the castle,
> And called it Rougemont at which name I started :
> Because a bard of Ireland told me once,
> I should not live long after I saw Richmond."

The castle was considerably injured a few years later when Perkin Warbeck, at the head of his Cornishmen, attacked the city. The fight seems to have been a long and furious one. The North Gate was burned, and both there and at the East Gate the rebels were temporarily successful. But after the Earl of Devon and his retinue came to the help of the citizens the rebels were expelled and had to make their way to Taunton, unsuccessful. Henry soon afterwards arrived bringing Perkin Warbeck with him. By his clemency towards the rebels he created real enthusiasm, so that the prisoners "hurled away their halters and cried God Save the King."

By the time Charles I. came to the throne the castle was already showing "gaping chinks and an aged countenance."

ROUGEMONT CASTLE.

Fairfax and his Roundheads completed the ruin. But it was not war only which left the building as we now see it. An ivy-covered gateway is all that remains. Yet from its summit one has a fine view of the surrounding country, and can readily

THE GUILDHALL, EXETER.

understand of what strategical value its possession must have been in "battles long ago."

The hand of the reformer proved stronger than that of the victorious captain. What war had failed to do enterprising citizens accomplished in times of peace. About the year 1770 the city fathers seem to have been animated by an unholy passion for destruction. Not only was the house of the Earls of Bedford, a house full of historic and majestic memories, pulled down, but the venerable fortress attracted attention. First a gateway, then the chapel, later the castellan's house disappeared. New assize courts, superlatively ugly, proudly rose in their stead. But even then the zeal of the reformers was not satiated. "Ten years later the Eastern Gate, with its two mighty flanking towers soaring over the picturesque house on each side with its wide and lofty Tudor arch spanning the road, its statue of Henry the Seventh, commemorating its rebuilding after the siege by Perkin Warbeck—the gate which was heir to that through which the conqueror made his way—all perished, to the great satisfaction of the Exeter of that day: for 'a beautiful vista was opened from St. Sidwell's into the High Street, a very great and necessary improvement.'" It is easy to share Professor Freeman's indignation; less easy, unhappily, to persuade men of our own day to deal kindly by the ancient monuments that are still left to us.

Another building that has played a notable part in the history of the city is the **Guildhall**, of which the portico makes so pleasing an ornament to the High Street. The building is a picturesque medley, "English windows and Italian pillars," and Professor Freeman wittily suggests that it serves to remind us of the jumble of tongues characterizing "much of the law business that has been done within it." The present building was built in 1464, replacing one of earlier date. There are many pictures of local interest in the hall, and also a portrait of Princess Henrietta Maria, who was born at Bedford House and christened in the cathedral. There seems to have been at one time a guild or confraternity connected with the chapel of St. George, erected over the hall about the last year of Richard III. In the accounts are found entries such as this, "Principae and others for exequis and masses said in the chapel of Guildhall for the repose of the souls for the brothers and sisters of the fraternity of St. George."

When Richard III. was nearing the end of his reign, the roof was fortified by a gun placed in charge of John Croker and ten soldiers. It is a strange coincidence that the chapel should have been built at this time. Evidently the wise citizens were determined to protect their interests both here and hereafter.

REFERENCES TO PLAN.

A. B. West Doors.
C. The Nave.
D, D. Nave Aisles.
E. Chapel of St. Edmund.
F. North Porch.
G. Transept North (St. Paul's Tower).
H. Chapel of St. John the Baptist.
I. Canon's Vestry.
J. The Choir.
K. K. Choir Aisles.
L. Syke's Chantry.
M. Chapel of St. James.
N. Chapel of St. George (Speke's Chantry).
O. Chapel of St. Saviour (Bishop Oldham's Chantry).
P. Lady Chapel.
Q. Chapel of St. Mary Magdalen.
R. Chapel of St. Gabriel.
T. Transept South (St. Peter's Tower).
U. Chapel of the Holy Ghost.
V. The Chapter House.
V. St. Paul's Chapel (North Transept).

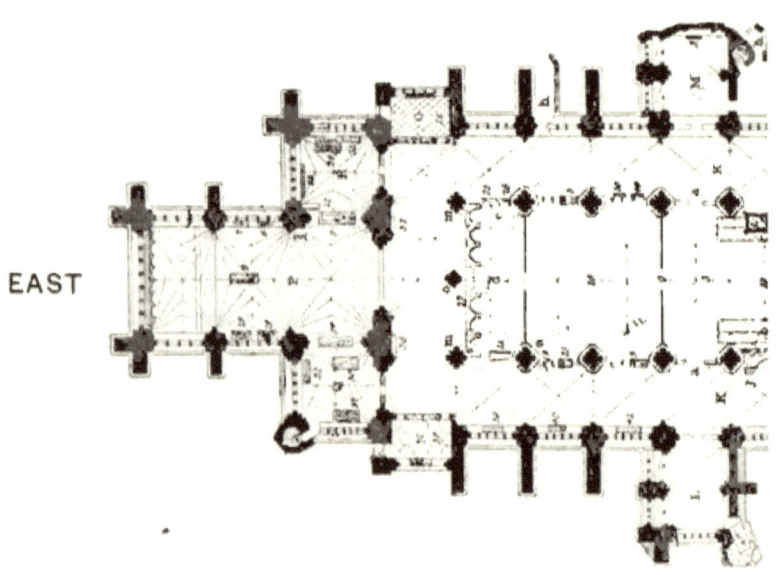

EAST

PLAN OF EXETER CATHEDRAL

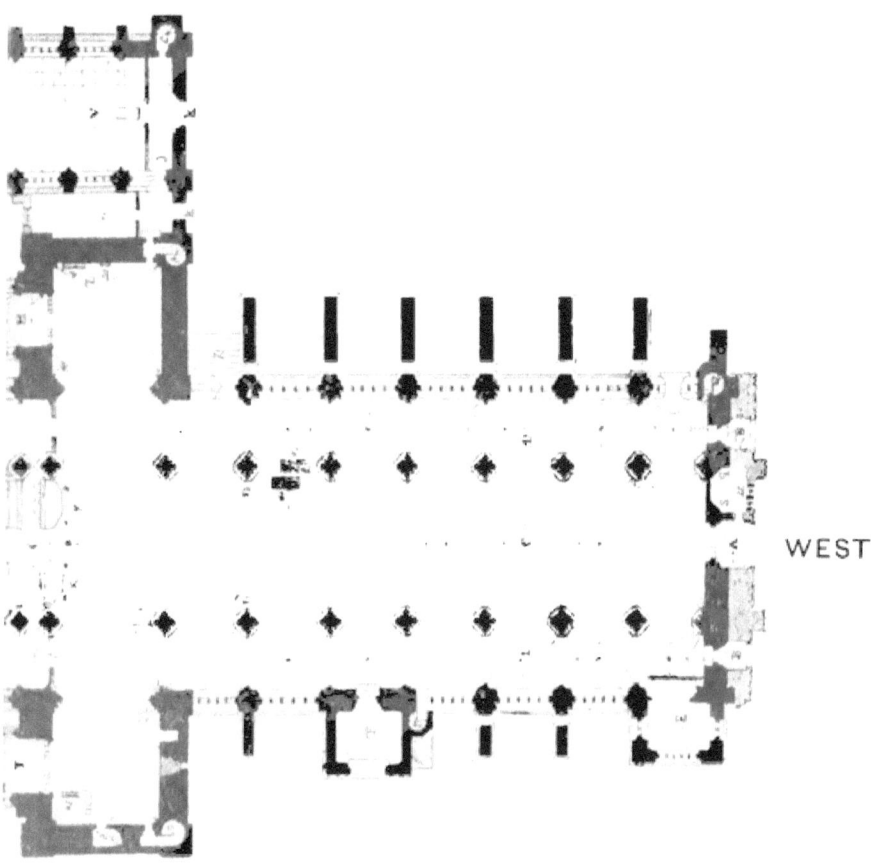

Bell's Cathedral Series.

EDITED BY
GLEESON WHITE AND E. F. STRANGE.

In specially designed cloth covers, crown 8vo, 1s. 6d. each.

Now Ready.

CANTERBURY. By HARTLEY WITHERS. 2nd Edition, revised. 36 Illustrations.
SALISBURY. By GLEESON WHITE. 2nd Edition, revised. 50 Illustrations.
CHESTER. By CHARLES HIATT. 24 Illustrations.
ROCHESTER. By G. H. PALMER, B.A. 38 Illustrations.
OXFORD. By Rev. PERCY DEARMER, M.A. 34 Illustrations.
EXETER. By PERCY ADDLESHAW, B.A. 35 Illustrations.
WINCHESTER. By P. W. SERGEANT. 50 Illustrations.
LICHFIELD. By A. B. CLIFTON. 42 Illustrations.
NORWICH. By C. H. B. QUENNELL. 38 Illustrations.
PETERBOROUGH. By Rev. W. D. SWEETING. 51 Illustrations.
HEREFORD. By A. HUGH FISHER. 34 Illustrations.

In the Press.

LINCOLN. By A. B. KENDRICK, B.A. | GLOUCESTER. By H. L. MASSÉ.
DURHAM. By J. E. BYGATE. | YORK. By A. CLUTTON BROCK, B.A.
WELLS. By Rev. PERCY DEARMER, M.A.

Preparing.

ST DAVID'S. By PHILIP ROBSON. WORCESTER. By E. F. STRANGE.
ELY. By T. D. ATKINSON. | SOUTHWELL. By Rev. ARTHUR DIMOCK.
CHICHESTER. CARLISLE. ST PAUL'S.
ST ALBANS. RIPON. BRISTOL.

Uniform with above Series.

BEVERLEY MINSTER. By CHARLES HIATT. *Preparing.*

Opinions of the Press.

"For the purpose at which they aim they are admirably done, and there are few visitors to any of our noble shrines who will not enjoy their visit the better for being furnished with one of these delightful books, which can be slipped into the pocket and carried with ease, and is yet distinct and legible. . . . A volume such as that on Canterbury is exactly what we want, and on our next visit we hope to have it with us. It is thoroughly helpful, and the views of the fair city and its noble cathedral are beautiful. Both volumes, moreover, will serve more than a temporary purpose, and are trustworthy as well as delightful." — *Notes and Queries.*

"We have so frequently in these columns urged the want of cheap, well-illustrated, and well-written handbooks to our cathedrals, to take the place of the out-of-date publications of local booksellers, that we are glad to hear that they have been taken in hand by Messrs George Bell & Sons." — *St James's Gazette.*

"Visitors to the cathedral cities of England must often have felt the need of some work dealing with the history and antiquities of the city itself, and the architecture and associations of the cathedral, more portable than the elaborate monographs which have been devoted to some of them, more scholarly and satisfying than the average local guide-book, and more copious than the section devoted to them in the general guide-book of the county or district. Such a legitimate need the 'Cathedral Series' now being issued by Messrs George Bell & Sons, under the editorship of Mr

Gleeson White and Mr E. F. Strange, seems well calculated to supply. The volumes are handy in size, moderate in price, well illustrated, and written in a scholarly spirit. The history of cathedral and city is intelligently set forth and accompanied by a descriptive survey of the building in all its detail. The illustrations are copious and well selected, and the series bids fair to become an indispensable companion to the cathedral tourist in England."—*Times.*

"They are nicely produced in good type, on good paper, and contain numerous illustrations, are well written, and very cheap. We should imagine architects and students of architecture will be sure to buy the series as they appear, for they contain in brief much valuable information."—*British Architect.*

"Half the charm of this little book on Canterbury springs from the writer's recognition of the historical association of so majestic a building with the fortunes, destinies, and habits of the English people. . . . One admirable feature of the book is its artistic illustrations. They are both lavish and satisfactory—even when regarded with critical eyes."—*Speaker.*

"There is likely to be a large demand for these attractive handbooks."—*Globe.*

"Bell's 'Cathedral Series,' so admirably edited, is more than a description of the various English cathedrals. It will be a valuable historical record, and a work of much service also to the architect. The illustrations are well selected, and in many cases not mere bald architectural drawings but reproductions of exquisite stone fancies, touched in their treatment by fancy and guided by art."—*Star.*

"Each of them contains exactly that amount of information which the intelligent visitor, who is not a specialist, will wish to have. The disposition of the various parts is judiciously proportioned, and the style is very readable. The illustrations supply a further important feature; they are both numerous and good. A series which cannot fail to be welcomed by all who are interested in the ecclesiastical buildings of England."—*Glasgow Herald.*

"Those who, either for purposes of professional study or for a cultured recreation, find it expedient to 'do' the English cathedrals will welcome the beginning of Bell's 'Cathedral Series.' This set of books is an attempt to consult, more closely, and in greater detail than the usual guide-books do, the needs of visitors to the cathedral towns. The series cannot but prove markedly successful. In each book a business-like description is given of the fabric of the church to which the volume relates, and an interesting history of the relative diocese. The books are plentifully illustrated, and are thus made attractive as well as instructive. They cannot but prove welcome to all classes of readers interested either in English Church history or in ecclesiastical architecture."—*Scotsman.*

"A set of little books which may be described as very useful, very pretty, and very cheap . . . . and alike in the letterpress, the illustrations, and the remarkably choice binding, they are ideal guides."—*Liverpool Daily Post.*

"They have nothing in common with the almost invariably wretched local guides save portability, and their only competitors in the quality and quantity of their contents are very expensive and mostly rare works, each of a size that suggests a packing-case rather than a coat-pocket. The 'Cathedral Series' are important compilations concerning history, architecture, and biography, and quite popular enough for such as take any sincere interest in their subjects."—*Sketch.*

LONDON: GEORGE BELL AND SONS.

www.ingramcontent.com/pod-product-compliance
Lightning Source LLC
Chambersburg PA
CBHW022136160426
43197CB00009B/1317